THE WORLD OF THE AGGADAH

Avigdor Shinan

THE WORLD OF
THE AGGADAH

MOD Books   Tel-Aviv

THE WORLD OF THE AGGADAH
by
Dr. AVIGDOR SHINAN
Senior Lecturer, Department of Hebrew Literature
Hebrew University, Jerusalem

Broadcast University Series
Galei Zahal — Tel Aviv University
Series Editor: Tirza Yuval

English translation by John Glucker

English Series Editor: Shmuel Himelstein

ISBN 965-05-0497-4

Computerized phototypesetting & printing: Naidat Press Ltd.
Printed in Israel

MOD Books — P.O.B. 7103, Tel-Aviv 61070, ISRAEL

In Memory of my Father, Yehudah Shinan, of Blessed Memory, Departed Rosh Hodesh Tammuz 5745

Contents

INTRODUCTION

The aggadic literature of our Sages, which was composed primarily in Eretz Israel in the first centuries of the Common Era, is not an isolated literary creation. It is like a many-branched, majestic tree: its roots reach down to the Biblical period, its leaves and shoots extend far into the Middle Ages, and its trunk, which lies at its heart, sends forth branches, some thick and others thin, in every direction, into the literary and cultural worlds contemporary with the Sages.

I set myself two goals in this book. The first was to describe briefly the main literatures and cultures which came into contact with the aggadic literature of our Sages, both internally — among the Jewish people — and externally. The other goal was to indicate the varied links and ties between the aggadic literature of the Sages and the worlds with which they came into contact, and also incidentally to give the reader an idea of the questions with which the scholars of the rabbinic literature deal. I have accompanied the discussion with many examples, chosen primarily because I believe they are of interest and are enjoyable.

I have naturally utilized numerous books and studies, most of them in Hebrew, but the framework in which these lectures were delivered did not enable me to acknowledge everyone whose work has been of assistance. For the English-speaking reader, a number of basic English sources germane to this area are listed in the bibliography at the end of the work.

The World of the Aggadah

I have had a number of faithful partners in this work:

— Tirzah Yuval, editor of this series for *Galei Zahal*, Israel Army Radio, who initiated it and aided in its implementation;

— My father, the late Yehudah Shinan, who listened to the lectures, criticized and praised them, and urged me to publish them;

— The Hebrew University, within whose walls I was able to prepare the text for publication;

— The publications department of the Ministry of Defence, which saw fit to publish the book first in Hebrew and now in English translation.

I owe all of them a debt of thanks and appreciation.

Avigdor Shinan
Rosh Ha-Shanah 5747

I.

The Aggadic Literature in Babylon and Eretz Israel

(In lieu of an introduction to the entire lecture series)

Halakhah has a stern countenance, aggadah has a cheerful countenance. The former is demanding, stringent, as hard as iron, the quality of strict justice; the latter is forgiving, lenient, as smooth as oil, the quality of mercy ... On the one hand, petrifying observance, obligation, servitude ... and on the other, constant renewal, freedom, liberty ... On the one hand — the dryness of prose, a firm and fixed style, gray, monotonous language, the rule of the intellect. And on the other hand — the vitality of poetry, a flowing, changing style, multi-hued language, the rule of the emotion.

It was in these words that the poet Hayyim Nahman Bialik, in his *Halakhah and Aggadah*, described the difference between the two major creative branches of the Sages — the halakhah and the aggadah. We will deal here with the cheerful countenance of this creation, the aggadic literature, our major aim being to review the literary and cultural world which *encompassed* the aggadic literature of our Sages: that which preceded it in time, that contemporary to it, and that which followed after it. The review will attempt to illustrate the links between the aggadic world of our Sages and the other literatures and cultures which surrounded it.

11

From this, one can understand that the literature of the Sages is not in itself the major concern of this work, but the world in which it was created and existed.

At the same time, it is advisable to have a few words of introduction to clarify the terms "the aggadic literature" and "our Sages," and we will begin with the latter.

The Hebrew term, *Hazal*, which we have translated as "our Sages," is in reality an acronym for the phrase, *Hakhamenu Zikhram li-Verakhah*, "Our Sages, may their memory be for a blessing." It is a relatively late term used to refer to a small group of people, some hundreds or a few thousand, the Torah sages of the Jewish people, who lived primarily in Eretz Israel and in Babylon approximately between the first to the seventh centuries of the Common Era. This chronological framework, I would venture to say, begins with Hillel the Elder, who lived close to the beginning of the Common Era, and ends with the first generations after the rise of Islam (close to 635 C.E.) in the Middle East.

The literary creations of our Sages were varied: They established for the Jewish people their halakhic — Jewish law — system (especially as found in the Mishnah and the Talmuds), formulated the *siddur* (prayer book) and composed *piyyutim* or liturgical hymns, interpreted the Bible in various ways and translated it into Aramaic, and also contributed to the aggadic literature, which is the focus of this work.

But what is aggadah? What does the word "aggadah" mean, and how is one to define it? Truth to tell, no adequate explanation has yet been found of this term, and various views have been expressed about its meaning. There are those who link it to the verb root HGD, i.e., to say, as opposed to *Mikra*, the word used for the Bible, the latter word being derived from the verb root KRA, meaning to read. Thus, while the Bible is meant to be read, the aggadah is meant to be related orally. Others see the word aggadah (again from the root HGD) as being in contrast to the word "halakhah": Halakhah implies walking (from the verb root HLKh), doing, carrying out an action, while aggadah is but speech, without any need to carry out any action of any kind. And yet again there are those who see the word "aggadah" as being derived from the verb root AGD, which means to gather together, to collect, and they understand it as meaning a collection or accumulation of different sayings. There are some that go even further afield and regard the word as being derived from the Aramaic verb root NGD, which means to pull or attract, and they explain the word aggadah as something which draws or attracts man's heart.

Those who offer the last opinion are somewhat correct: the aggadah does indeed attract the heart; but they are mistaken in their etymology, for it is difficult to regard this Aramaic verb root as being the basis for this word. We should note that most of the attempts to explain the word, as we saw above, are limited to the literature of our Sages. Yet we have in our possession, as we will see at length later, aggadic works which are much earlier than our Sages, as well as works after their era, and I feel that it is not correct to confine the term to the limits used by our Sages.

In brief: all speak of the aggadah or read the aggadic literature, even though the precise meaning of the word itself is not perfectly clear to us.

Even though we have not been able to explain the word etymologically, we may at least be able to define what the "aggadah" is. Yet, even here, things are not that simple. In the *Entsiklopedia Ivrit* ("Hebrew Encyclopedia"), for example, aggadah (and here we refer to that of our Sages) is defined negatively: "That part of the oral law [i,e., primarily the literature of the Sages] that is not halakhah," but the fact that this is defined negatively only shows how difficult it is to find a positive definition of the term, a definition which will state clearly what the aggadah is, and will not hide behind other terms such as "halakhah" or "the oral law." A similar attempt to define the aggadah was made by the distinguished aggadah scholar, Yom-Tov Lippmann (Leopold) Zunz (1794—1886), father of Wissenschaft des Judentums in the 19th century, who stated that "whatever one can imagine is to be found in the aggadah, except for one thing: frivolity and flippancy" (and, of course, except for halakhah). This definition would include interpretations on the Bible, tales of the Sages and their disciples, ethical works, parables, poetry, prayers, hyperbole, jokes, medical discussions, geography, astrology, biology, folk tales, incantations and witchcraft, words of consolation and messianic promises, historic documents, theological deliberations, and so on. In other words, if we wish to offer a positive definition of aggadah, we would have to enumerate all those creative areas which are not halakhah, and even a long and detailed list would have to end with the words, "and so on," in order not to exclude anything we might have inadvertently left out. Here too, we should again note that both Zunz and the *Entsiklopedia Ivrit* only attempted to define the aggadic literature of our Sages, but aggadic literature had been created among the Jewish people even before the era of our Sages, and it is possible that the definition will be somewhat different.

Here we must admit that many excellent people deal with the aggadah regularly without being able to explain clearly what the word means, and without being able to define it concisely and clearly in a positive fashion. One can console himself with the fact that, at least intuitively, we more or less understand what is meant, and the question is not as problematic as it appears to be.

The aggadic literature of our Sages, if we return to our subject, refers to the aggadic works of our Sages created between the first to the seventh centuries of the Common Era. In this lecture series we will, as mentioned, examine the world which surrounded this literature and will therefore extend our survey beyond the centuries in which our Sages lived, for their aggadic literature — as we have stressed and explained — is but a part, even if it is the major part, of Jewish aggadic creativity in various periods. *Chronologically*, we will thus deal with texts which were composed during a long period of time, going back to about 330 B.C.E. — the time that the East and the civilized world were conquered by Alexander the Great — and extending to about the 13th or the 14th century C.E., more than 1,500 years of literary creativity. At the beginning of the period with which we are dealing there was a decisive cultural and political revolution in the entire world: Greek culture met the Eastern (and Semitic) cultures. These together formed a new entity which signified the beginning of a new era, the Hellenistic era. It was at that time that the complex and lengthy process of the canonization of the Bible took place, and everything created by the Jewish people after this time (except for a few works which still managed to be included in the Bible) is considered to be post-Biblical, and belongs to either halakhah or aggadah. The period of the 13th or 14th centuries was chosen as the concluding era for this study because at that time various people composed comprehensive and summary works of the aggadic literature, these being the different *Yalkutim* (such as *Yalkut Shimoni* among the German Jews or *Ha-Midrash ha-Gadol* of the Yemenite Jews). In these works, the authors attempted to include in a single collection all the aggadic literature of which they were aware, and their work may be regarded as somewhat of a canonization of the aggadic literature. Chronologically, we will thus deal with the period between these two eras — that of the canonization of the Bible and that of the "canonization," as it were, of the aggadah.

Geographically, we will not concentrate only on the center in Eretz Israel, but will investigate what was created in the aggadic literature in Babylon in the northeast, in Alexandria in the south, and even in various Hellenistic colonies in North Africa and Asia Minor. Other works that will be mentioned were edited in Europe — primarily in Greece, Italy and Germany — and in Yemen.

We will also range widely in examining *the literary genres*. We will discuss works which explain or retell the stories of the Bible, translations of the Bible, *piyyutim* — liturgical poems — as well as mystical, polemical and historiographical works. We will also come across works which belong to the wisdom literature and even ancient plays written about Biblical themes. In short, we will review a very wide range of literary genres, will encompass many geographical regions and will deal with an extended time span, and at the center of all of these we will discuss the aggadic literature of our Sages.

We will also extend our study beyond the Jewish framework. We will deal with a number of cultures which were close to the Jewish culture of those times, and which have a certain literary and cultural link with the aggadic literature of our Sages. I refer here to the

Christian literature, to that of the Samaritans, and to Islamic culture. In regard to each of the three, we will ask what it can contribute to a better understanding of the Jewish aggadic works.

One of the details mentioned above appears to me to need special attention, and it is on this that the rest of this chapter will focus.

The aggadic literature of our Sages is primarily an Eretz Israel literature, and those who believe that most of the aggadah of our Sages was created in Babylon — and is embedded in the Babylonian Talmud — are mistaken. This common misconception stems from the fact that the Babylonian Talmud, of all the works by our Sages, was the most commonly studied work in the Middle Ages. In all Jewish communities, the Talmud was the major work from which our fathers knew the words of our Sages, and this detracted from the status of the various aggadic and halakhic midrashim. The impression was therefore created that most of the aggadah is to be found in the Babylonian Talmud. A series of books written by the scholar Wilhelm Bacher (1850—1913) at the beginning of this century has proved conclusively that this impression is erroneous.

Bacher wished to write a series of books which would include all "the aggadot of the Tanna'im" (i.e., those sages who lived in Eretz Israel between the period of Hillel the Elder and the completion of the Mishnah by R' Judah the Patriarch, in about 200 C.E.), "the aggadot of the Amora'im of Eretz Israel" and "the aggadot of the Amora'im of Babylon" (the Amora'im were those sages who lived after the completion of the Mishnah and were active in two different centers, Babylon and Eretz Israel, and there developed their teachings). Bacher decided to publish a series of books containing the aggadic material, classified into three groups according to the names of the sages involved. As he worked though, he found, possibly to his own great surprise, that the aggadic material created by the Amora'im of Babylon contained only enough to fill a slim volume, while the material created by the Amora'im of Eretz Israel (and before them, the Tanna'im) was many times as large.

It appears that even within the Babylonian Talmud itself the majority of aggadot originated in Eretz Israel, as is apparent from their language, their content, or the names of the sages transmitting them, and thus the Babylonian Talmud itself testifies to the wealth of the Eretz Israel aggadah. It would thus appear that individuals that wandered from the Eretz Israel center to Babylon brought the Eretz Israel Torah to Babylon (and back), and their actions contributed to the optical illusion that the Babylonian Talmud is the major aggadic work of our Sages.

Can we explain this fact? Why was the aggadic literature composed primarily in Eretz Israel? Many great scholars have dealt with this question, and at least four theories have been propounded. On this, we should adopt a basic principle: When various answers are offered to a single question, it is possible that we can only obtain a correct and full answer if we combine all or some of the answers into one.

The first answer to the question of the almost exclusively Eretz Israel origin of the aggadic literature is based on the assumption that the aggadic literature was conceived and created primarily as the result of the spiritual struggle of the creators of the aggadah among themselves or between them and foreign beliefs and views and other cultures. Now we know that Eretz Israel, throughout almost the entire time that we will be dealing with, from the 3rd century B.C.E. to the Crusader era, was the scene of cultural tensions and struggles. Thus there were internal struggles, such as those between the School of Hillel and the School of Shammai, or, earlier, between the Hellenists and the Zealots; as well as the external struggles between the Jews of Eretz Israel and Hellenism, the Samaritans, or sectarian cults such as the Dead Sea Sect (to which we will devote a separate lecture), or the sect which began as a Jewish one and later became known as Christianity (and we will deal with this separately as well). These struggles were also accompanied by conflicts with a foreign and hostile government — such as Rome, and later Byzantium and Islam — and, according to this view, it is these that nourished the aggadic literature in Eretz Israel and inspired the creation of many aggadot. As to the other great Jewish center during our Sages' era, Babylon (the holders of this view will contend) — which was also under foreign rule — the

Jews generally lived untroubled lives, and the government did not usually become excessively involved in the internal lives of its subjects. Thus, as opposed to Eretz Israel, where the Jews were constantly involved in serious conflict, the Babylonian Jews lived, of course relatively, in peace and tranquility. In Babylon there was greater religious toleration and openness, and there was no severe and cruel religious persecution. The Jews of Babylon therefore did not need to direct their spiritual resources as diligently to the aggadah.

Let us take an example of an aggadah that was created as part of a polemical struggle, and without that as the background it will be difficult to understand this aggadah fully. This aggadah deals with the story of the sacrifice of Isaac in the Book of Genesis. As we know, Abraham was told to go and sacrifice his son Isaac (Gen. 22:2) "on one of the mountains which I will tell you," but he was not told specifically which mountain it was to be. Later, we are told that Abraham (22:4) "saw the place from afar," and wished to fulfill God's command. The Midrash, rightfully, asks: "What did he see?" and how did Abraham know that the place which he saw was the one upon which he was to sacrifice Isaac? And the Midrash answers: "He saw a cloud attached to the mountain" — in other words, he was given a Divine revelation which informed him that this was the chosen mountain. (Incidentally, the word *makom* in the verse, which we translated above as "place" — the customary translation — is understood by the Midrash as a synonym — one used often in rabbinic literature — for God. Thus, the verse is interpreted as "he saw God from afar.") According to the Torah, Abraham and Isaac were accompanied by two young slaves. The Midrash therefore continues:

> He [i.e., Abraham] said: "It would appear that that is the place upon which the Holy One, blessed be, He commanded me to sacrifice my son." He said to Isaac: "My son, do you see what I do?" He told him, "Yes." He said to his two young men, "Do you see what I do?" They said to him, "No." He said: "As an ass does not see and you do not see, remain here with the ass." (*Midrash Bereshit Rabbah* 56:2).

Other sources state that Abraham added when speaking to his youths, "for you resemble an ass," and state that Gentiles as a rule are "a nation resembling an ass."

Now, logically, only in a place where there was a dispute as to whether there is such a thing as Divine revelation to non-Jews would there be cause for so forceful an aggadah, which states clearly that the non-Jew (represented here by Abraham's servants) is like a beast which is incapable of attaining Divine revelation. Only in a place where there were vehement arguments about the question of the ability of non-Jews to see the Divine Presence was there reason for the development of this clearly polemical midrash. This place was evidently Eretz Israel, in which there were acrimonious debates between the Christians and the Jews regarding the possibility of prophecy after the destruction of the Second Temple and the question of Divine revelation to one who was not Jewish. And it was evidently against the Christians that this midrash was directed, telling them, as it were: You are like asses that are incapable of seeing!

Here is another example of how polemics can create aggadot:

The straw, chaff and stubble were arguing among themselves. One said, "The field was planted for me," whereas the other said, "The field was planted for me." The wheat said to them: "Wait until the threshing time comes, and then we will know for whom the field was planted." The harvest time arrived. When the grain had been brought to the threshing floor, the owner went to winnow it. The chaff was carried away by the wind. [The owner] took the stubble and threw it to the ground. He took the straw and burned it. He took the wheat and made a heap of it (*Shir ha-Shirim Rabbah* 7:3).

Immediately after this parable, we find the moral:

The same is true with the (other) nations of the world. These say, "We are Israel, and the world was created for us," while these say, "We are Israel, and the world was created for us." Israel then said to them: "Wait until the day of the Holy One, blessed be He comes [i.e., the eschatological Day of Judgment]. and we will know for whom the world was created." (*Ibid.*)

19

It is not clear against whom this parable was directed. Was this against the Christians, who regarded themselves as Israel in spirit, the true Israel, or against the Samaritans, who had similar claims, or was it against both of them? In any event, whoever created this parable in the 3rd or 4th century C.E. was obviously attacking views current in his time. Where there are no polemics, such aggadot do not arise. The numerous aggadot which mock Rome, while portraying it as the Biblical Esau, also stem from the Jewish-Roman polemic, and this polemic was conducted in Eretz Israel, but not in Babylon.

To this point, we have given the first of the four answers as to why the aggadah was primarily an Eretz Israel creation. Now we come to another explanation, which although it may be a little naive, has a great deal of truth to it. According to this explanation, aggadah, just as poetry, is nurtured by the soil of one's homeland. The first *payyetanim* (i.e., those who wrote *piyyutim* — and we will yet deal with them) were all from Eretz Israel; until the beginning of the 10th century there was no real poetry of any significance, qualitatively or quantitatively, outside Eretz Israel and its sphere of influence. Indeed, we find that when the Levites were asked by their captors in Babylon to sing their songs, they responded: "How can we sing the song of the Lord on foreign soil?" (Ps. 137:4) There is evidently some type of internal and profound link between poetic creativity — and the aggadah is a special type of poetry — and a nation's living on its own soil. Even if we say that this view is somewhat simplistic, there is still justification from another point of view. Most of the aggadic traditions are linked to Eretz Israel and its different places: stories about the Temple Mount or the Cave of Machpelah, descriptions of miracles which took place for our forefathers in this or that place, stories about graves of Tanna'im and Amora'im, etc. These aggadot were preserved near these places from generation to generation, and sometimes were even developed and embellished further. In the far-off diaspora, such aggadot would not have been considered to be as essential, and, if preserved, would be preserved in their exact form, without further embellishments. This, then, is the second explanation why the aggadah was not developed in the diaspora, in Babylon, but in Eretz Israel.

A third explanation, which is of a sociological and historical nature, links aggadic creation to the historic, economic, and political situation in which its creators live. Bitter reality, say the holders of this view, forces people to flee to another world, an imaginary world where everything is good, one which brings comfort and encouragement in its wake. The condition of the Jews in Eretz Israel, throughout almost the entire time involved here, was deplorable, whereas in Babylon it was relatively good. Thus we are told clearly by R' Isaac, an Eretz Israel sage:

> At first, when money was available, a person would desire to hear something of the Mishnah or of the Talmud. Now that money is no longer available, and especially as we suffer from the government, a person wishes to hear something of the Bible or of the Aggadah (*Pesikta d'Rav Kahana* 12:3).

In this statement, R' Isaac links literary output to the economic and political situation. When money was available and people were able to support themselves easily, they had the time, the patience and the spiritual power to sit down and deal with the Mishnah and the Talmud, with the halakhic problem of an egg laid on *Yom Tov*, for example. Now that the Jews all lived in poverty and suffering, they sought refuge in fleeing to words of the Aggadah and to Biblical stories. With this as the background, we can also understand the elaborate descriptions of the World to Come and glowing pictures of the messianic times, as well as the "literary vengeance" taken by the members of that generation against their enemies, by means of the stories which mocked Esau (Rome) or Ishmael (Islam). Where a person seeks a refuge from reality, he flees to literature. This is the third explanation as to why the aggadah originated in Eretz Israel.

Now we come to the fourth explanation, which appears to be more logical than the others, but, as mentioned, it should be understood together with the others. This explanation is primarily psychological, and is based on the recognition of the fact that the people of Babylon regarded the aggadah in a different light than did the people of Eretz Israel, for the people of the two countries had a different psychological make-up. "It is a tradition from my forefathers," states R' Johanan (also of Eretz Israel), "not to teach the aggadah to a Babylonian or to a southerner (i.e., those who lived in Lydda or to the south of that city), for they are coarse people and have little Torah" (Jerusalem Talmud *Pesahim* 5:3). R' Johanan thus regarded the Babylonians (and the southerners as well) as "coarse people," who were unable to understand the aggadot, which were often based on word play, which required the exercise of the imagination and which lent themselves to flights of imagination, and he therefore refused to teach them to these people.

And indeed, if one compares the Babylonian Talmud and the Jerusalem Talmud (the latter being the Talmud of those who lived in Eretz Israel) — and, as is known, the two works often cover the same tractates of the Mishnah — he will immediately see that the acuity of the Babylonian scholars exceeded that of the Eretz Israel scholars. But the same person who was able to erect imposing and complex edifices in halakhah was not capable of dealing with poetic and artistic works, as described here. In Babylon, they dealt with the aggadic material differently than they did in Eretz Israel. Only in Babylon, for example, do we find numerous attempts to reconcile contradictory aggadot or to harmonize aggadot which are not in keeping with one another. Only in Babylon do we find that they raised questions on aggadic statements and tried to answer them, or that they used aggadic thoughts for clearly halakhic purposes. The Babylonian scholars, so it would appear, were first and foremost interested in the halakhah, and even when they dealt with the aggadah, they dealt with it through the prism of the halakhah, using those tools suitable for halakhah.

These four views, and especially when they are taken together, can offer a satisfactory explanation for the Eretz Israel origin of the aggadic creation of our Sages, a creation whose overall world we will review in the coming chapters.

II.

The Apocryphal Literature

Every review of the aggadic literature which encompasses the literature of our Sages should rightfully begin with the Apocrypha and Pseudepigrapha. This collective term is generally used to connote a group of more than 30 works written by Jews, primarily in Eretz Israel, during the Second Temple era and in the first generations after the destruction of the Temple. This group (as well as a number of other works which were canonized in the Bible), represents, without a doubt, but a partial and accidental selection of the totality of books written among the Jewish people during the Second Temple era.

The non-Jewish scholar, when dealing with these books, generally divides then into two groups: the first is known as Apocrypha — a word which one might properly translate as "concealed," while the other is referred to as the Pseudepigrapha, which can be translated as "falsely attributed to," i.e., books where the writer, for reasons known to himself, prefers to attribute the authorship to someone else, in most cases a famous historic personality. But the two names are not particularly correct, because there are works which are part of the Apocrypha, but which are nevertheless "attributed to" various famous people, while on the other hand there are books which are part of the Pseudepigrapha which were "hidden" for a lengthy period of time. In reality the division of these books into two groups is really meant to distinguish between those books which were canonized in the Greek

The World of the Aggadah

version of the Bible, i.e., the Septuagint (which we will deal with below), and those books which were not included in it.

And this was the way things happened: at a certain time, the Hebrew (i.e., Jewish) Bible was canonized. (In order to simplify matters, henceforth any reference to "the Bible" will refer to the Jewish Bible, unless specified differently.) We do not know when this occurred and where it took place; nor do we know definitely who was responsible for the action, and what principles were used to determine the canonization — and that is without a doubt one of the most fascinating questions in the cultural history of the Jewish people. In any event, it is clear that in a certain place and at a certain time, someone or some people decided — and we are not sure if it was one individual, an official body, or various groups of people — that the Bible would include the present 24 books and no more. (The Jewish method of counting the books of the Bible considers both parts of Samuel to be a single book, and so too both parts of Kings and Chronicles. The twelve Minor Prophets are all considered to be a single book.) This was not a decision reached all at once, but was part of a long and complex process which was accompanied by disputes. We have but fragments of information about that process. We know, for example, that there were major disputes about the inclusion of certain specific books, such as the Song of Songs, which someone regarded as a secular poem not worthy of being canonized, whereas another considered it to be the "holy of holies," a love poem between God and His nation. There was also a major dispute about Ecclesiastes, some of whose statements were perceived as being heretical. Even the Book of Ezekiel was not accepted into the canon unequivocally, because there were found in it halakhic decisions which contradicted those in the Torah. In any event, the struggle finally came to an end, and 24 books were included in the canon, while the rest were thrust aside.

Those books not found suitable to be included in the canon are the basis for the Apocrypha, and that is indeed the source of their name in Hebrew, the *sefarim hitzoni'im* — "the external (or "outside") books," i.e., those books which are outside the canon of the Bible. These books, and others which were written later during

24

the Second Temple era, were naturally not considered to be Holy Writ; they were not copied, were not studied, and some of them were even forgotten over the course of time. Some of these books were obviously rejected because of the religious beliefs they express, others because of the peculiar halakhah they contain, but most of them were evidently rejected simply because of a principle which already appears in the Mishnah: "One who reads the *sefarim hitzoni'im* ... has no place in the World to Come" (*San.* 10:1). That is what R' Akiva stated, and by that statement he invalidated those books which were not found worthy of being included in the Biblical canon. Indeed, he may have stated what he did in order to strengthen the position of the Book of Books. In any event, most of the books which had been rejected were translated into the cultural language of the era, Greek — which was also the language of the largest Jewish diaspora of those days — and thus it came about that they were preserved in the writings of the Christian Church in various places and (after being translated mostly from Greek) in various languages, such as Latin, Syriac, Slavic, Armenian, and so on. Furthermore, as these books remained only in the Christian Church, they were often "improved upon," and changes were introduced freely by various Christian scribes who wished to make them correspond to what they considered to be proper doctrine.

Since the *haskalah* era, and primarily from the end of the previous century, when Abraham Kahana undertook his great project of returning these lost books to their original source, and for this purpose assembled a group of scholars who retranslated these works back to Hebrew, Jews have been able to read these works in their own language and to examine them, both in regard to the topics involved and their characteristics. Thus this chapter, in which I intend to list the major works in each group, will be devoted to the apocryphal works. I hope to comment on their importance, and, most particularly, to discuss their contribution to the research on the aggadic literature of our Sages.

★ ★ ★

We will first discuss the Apocrypha, i.e., those books canonized only in the Greek Bible, the Septuagint, which served as the basis for the

The World of the Aggadah

Christian Bible. Of this group of books, we will mention five works. Two of them will be dealt with relatively at length, and three will be mentioned only briefly.

The first of these books in terms of importance is that of Ben Sira. This was composed by a Jerusalem scribe, probably a priest, named Joshua (although there are versions which refer to him as Simeon) ben Sira, who lived at the end of the third century B.C.E., i.e., a few generations before the Hasmonean era, in a period of Jewish history of which we know almost nothing. As far as literary form and content, the book is very similar to Proverbs and to parts of Ecclesiastes, and its major concern is generally that of wisdom and morals. Below are two examples taken from the Book of Ben Sira (and one should note how difficult it is to differentiate between his words and those of the canonical Wisdom Literature). In one place, Ben Sira states: "A fool will raise his voice in frivolity / and a clever man will laugh delicately" (21:22). In other words, one can tell from a person's laughter if he is a fool or a wise man. So too, on an entirely different topic, he declares: "It is better to dwell with a lion and a dragon / than to dwell with an evil woman" (25:19). Incidentally, there are other places as well that the author expresses unsympathetic comments about women, and it is generally accepted that his own life was what caused him to adopt this anti-feminist view.

The Sages evidently knew the Book of Ben Sira, and this is one of those works which was not lost completely when it was not found worthy of canonization. Until a relatively late time, even in the 3rd and 4th centuries C.E. — i.e., about 600 years after it was written — it was still being quoted by our Sages, who used expressions in reference to it which are generally reserved for quotes from the Bible. This shows that for a long time the Book of Ben Sira was considered to be on the border line between the canonical works and the apocryphal ones, and only in a relatively late era was it finally decided that it was not worthy of being included in the canon. It is therefore not surprising that passages from Ben Sira (and in the Hebrew original!) are to be found among the writings of different Jewish sects, such as in those of the Dead Sea Sect and at Massada, as well as in the famous Cairo Genizah.

It is worth paying special attention to the last chapters of the book, Chapters 44—48. This section is referred to as "Praise of the Fathers of the Universe," and gives a description of the forefathers of the Jewish people from Enoch to Nehemiah, according to the Biblical order, while adding praises for each individual. Thus, for example, we read of Joshua bin Nun:

> A man of valor Joshua bin Nun / Servant of Moses in prophecy
>
> Who was created to be in his days / A great salvation for his people
>
> To take vengeance of the enemy / And to have Israel gain their inheritance
>
> How glorious when he stretched forth a hand / When he raised up a javelin on a city
>
> Who can withstand him / For he fought the battles of the Lord. (46:1—4)

Ben Sira devotes a great deal of space to Aaron, but that is not remarkable, because, after all, the author was a priest from Jerusalem, who regarded himself as one of Aaron's descendants.

The major source for Ben Sira's comments, is, of course, the Bible. But he adds to this various post-Biblical fragments of tradition. Thus, for example, he says about Enoch, one of the individuals between Adam and Noah: "Enoch was found to be pure (*tamim* in Hebrew) and walked before God and was taken / A sign from generation to generation" (44:16). What is important to our discussion is the use of the word *tamim*. From this we can see that, in the 3rd century B.C.E., as stated by this Jerusalem author, Enoch was considered to be a positive character. This fact is interesting, because in a later Jewish tradition, such as in *Bereshit Rabbah* (25:1), Enoch is included among the flatterers and the wicked, who were taken before their time in order not to harm mankind. Yet Ben Sira, hundreds of years earlier, gives a different view, one which regards Enoch favorably. Thus Ben Sira helps us to describe the development that Enoch's image underwent in the post-Biblical era. Had we not been aware of Ben Sira, we would have assumed

that the midrashic statement reflects the general view of post–
Biblical Judaism.

Another book in the Apocrypha is Judith. According to a number
of scholars it was written during the Persian era, i.e., before the
Hellenistic era of the 4th century B.C.E. The book was definitely
written in Hebrew and in Eretz Israel. This is the story: A woman
named Judith, who was a rich, beautiful and pious widow and who
lived in an evidently fictitious town named Betuliah, came to the aid
of her people when the enemy (Assyria), led by its military
commander, Holofernes, went to war against the Jews. Judith came
to Holofernes, and during a feast, when he was drunk, she
persuaded him to seclude himself with her. She promptly beheaded
him and returned to her city, with his head wrapped in the folds of
her cloak. This is a simple tale and one can see in it the influence of
various Biblical stories, such as that of Yael and Sisera or of David
and Goliath. Scholars believe that the book has a very shaky historic
base, and its major moral is its display of heroism and of perfect
faith in God. It offers encouragement in times of distress, a call for
faith in God and for observance of His commandments. When the
fathers of the 4th century B.C.E. wished to educate their children,
this story served them admirably.

We will also make brief mention of three other books of the
Apocrypha. These include the Books of Maccabees (or of the
Hasmoneans), which are the most important source available to us
about that era. Another delightful book is that of Susannah: a story
with a pleasant plot and a clear moral, of a beautiful and modest
woman who was coveted by two evil old men. These men falsely
accused Susannah of having committed adultery and thus caused
her to be sentenced to death. Daniel, a wise youth, proved that the
men were lying, and thus Susannah was ruled innocent. This group
also includes an addition to the Book of Esther, containing a dream
dreamed by Mordecai, in which he was told what would happen in
the future, etc.

From all of this, one can see the broad range of literature which existed
at the time of the Second Temple — historic descriptions, additions
to the Bible, collections of wise sayings, and various types of stories.

The second group of works, the Pseudepigrapha, includes about twenty works that were not included in the Bible nor in the Septuagint. Here too we will only mention five — two at length and three briefly.

One of the important works in this group is The Testaments of the Twelve Tribes (or: The Testaments of the Sons of Jacob), which was evidently written during the Hasmonean period. It consists of twelve chapters, each of which is constructed as the testament written by one of Jacob's sons. Before their deaths, the twelve sons tell their descendants, in the first person, of the events of their lives and confess their sins, sometimes including their role in the sale of Joseph, or point out their good deeds, and command their children to act in this way or that. Sometimes their words are intertwined with "prophecies" about the future, in which Jacob's sons tell their children (and the reader) what will happen in the future. The work was definitely written in Jewish circles, but reached us in Christian versions, and the latter made sure to add — especially in regard to the tribe of Judah, from whom the messiah will come — various "prophecies" about Jesus. The reader of this book thus needs to exert great effort if he wishes to ascertain its Jewish source.

Below are two examples of what one can find in this work: In the testament attributed to Judah, there is a very long description of the war of Jacob and his sons against the Canaanites (a topic which has but the most vague of allusions in the Torah). The description goes into great length and is full of gory details, including beheadings and brutal acts of murder, such as:

> The king of Tapu'ah, who rode a horse, I [and we remember that this refers to Judah himself] killed ... as well as the king of Ahor, a giant, whom I found shooting arrows and heaving a rock weighing sixty pounds ... and I killed him with the horse. I fought Aher for two hours and I killed him as well, and I cleaved his shield into two parts and cut off his legs. As I removed his armor, eight of his friends came to attack me ... I stoned them and killed four of them, and the rest fled. (3:2—6)

And so on and so forth. There are four complete chapters which include chronicles of war of this type.

29

The World of the Aggadah

This reminds us somewhat of the Book of Judith, with the glorification of acts of physical bravery and an indication of the value of the use of physical force. This is possibly one of the characteristics of the Second Temple literature, as opposed to the literature of our Sages. It would appear that, following the failure of the great revolt, and especially after the collapse of Bar Kokhba's revolt — a traumatic blow which brought about a terrible bloodbath in its wake — the Sages decided to reject this type of literature and such descriptions, and, as opposed to this, to stress the spiritual and religious values of Judaism. Thus, for example, in the literature of our Sages, the mighty man of the Bible, Samson, becomes a wise scholar who studies Torah in a yeshivah, and Jacob's words, where he indicates that he conquered Shechem with his sword and his bow (see Gen. 48:22), are interpreted or translated to indicate that he received the city through his request and prayer to God; and the verse is thus regarded as a prayer to God rather than an indication of the use of physical force.

Another topic which recurs in the testaments is the story of the sale of Joseph. And here we have an interesting phenomenon: a number of brothers tell of their involvement in the sale of Joseph, but each regards it from his own particular vantage point, and it is interesting to compare a number of different views of the same situation. Thus, for example, Zebulun says to his sons, while declaring himself completely innocent of any wrongdoing:

> And with the money from the sale [of Joseph] I had no part, because Simeon and Dan and Gad and their children took the sale money and used it to buy for themselves and their wives and children shoes ... And after they threw him into the pit, my brothers sat down to eat and to drink, and I did not taste a thing, for I pitied Joseph (Testament of Zebulun 3:1; 4:1—2).

Thus the teller relates the Biblical story anew, but this time from Zebulun's particular vantage point, which enriches the Biblical account considerably.

We should also note another detail of Zebulun's story: the money the other brothers received was used to buy shoes for them and their families. What is the origin of the author's strange tradition? It

30

would appear that the source of this is a special understanding of a verse in the Book of Amos, in which the prophet claims that the Jewish people sinned (2:6), "because they sold the righteous for silver, and the poor for a pair of shoes." I do not know exactly what the prophet meant, but already in the 2nd century B.C.E. this verse was interpreted as referring to the sale of Joseph (the righteous) for shoes. If that is so, we have an ancient midrash, among the most ancient, which predates the literature of our Sages by hundreds of years and repeats this story motif. The Books of Testaments thus enables us, with quite a bit of certainty, to date the time when this aggadic tradition was formed.

Another work in this group is The Book of Jubilees, which was preserved in Ethiopian. This book comes ostensibly to fill a lacuna in the Torah regarding Moses. As we know, Moses went up on Mount Sinai and remained there for forty days and forty nights, but what did he do during all that time? According to The Book of Jubilees, Moses met one of the angels on Mount Sinai, and the latter told him, in great detail, the history of the world from its creation until his times, with extensive elaborations on the Biblical accounts, while filling in many gaps and expanding on various stories. This book, too, was evidently written during the Hasmonean period, and what makes it unique — and this is also the explanation of its name — is the way it enumerates the dates of events recorded in it. According to this work, history is divided into jubilees of seven times seven years, and not into decades or centuries, as we would do. Incidentally, the halakhah as reflected in this work is unique and exceptional, and that was certainly one of the reasons that the book was rejected and was not accepted into the Jewish tradition.

Thus, for example, the author of The Book of Jubilees states:

> In the sixtieth year of Abraham's life ... Abraham got up at night and burned the house of idolatry [belonging to his father], and he burned everything in the house, and no one knew. They arose that night and attempted to save their idols from the fire. Haran, Abraham's brother, ran to save them, and the fire engulfed him and he died in Ur of the Chaldees, during the life of his father, Terah (12:12—13).

31

The World of the Aggadah

The story of Abraham who smashed or burned his father's idols is very well known in Jewish tradition, but it would appear that this story appeared for the first time neither in *Rashi's* commentary nor in the Midrash, but much earlier, before the destruction of the Temple. From this point of view — but not only from this point of view — these works are very important, in supplying us, as we mentioned, with guidelines for dating the traditions.

What one must realize is that one of the biggest problems in research on the literature of our Sages is the question of the time during which a certain aggadic tradition was created. For example, when was the idea formulated that Abraham burned (or destroyed) his father's idols? When did the tradition of the brothers selling Joseph for shoes, of all things, originate? In most cases, it is very difficult to obtain a clear answer from the literature of our Sages. Statements wander from one sage to another, from one period to another, and from one work to another. Furthermore, many statements are anonymous and one cannot always tell who fathered them. Generally, too, the statements offer us no means to identify what the historic background was at the time they were formulated. But the works which we have dealt with to now, such as Ben Sira or The Testaments, serve as an external dating tool, with whose aid we can offer a more accurate dating for various traditions, and, of course, an earlier dating, as all of the books mentioned in this chapter predate the literature of our Sages.

I will also mention briefly three other books of the Pseudepigrapha. One, Biblical Antiquities, which has been attributed to Philo (and we will still have more to say about this philosopher, who did not write this work) was written about the time of the destruction of the Second Temple, and reviews the history of the Jewish people from the creation of the world until the death of Saul. Another work is The Book of Enoch, which tells of what happened to Enoch in heaven, his voyage there and his meetings with those from far worlds. Another work is The Book of Adam and Eve, in which Eve gives her version of the roles of Adam and the snake in the story of that sin, and also gives her opinion of what happened there. She also includes in her words a discussion of the importance of repenting and even offers various "prophecies" about the future.

Let us summarize what we said in this chapter: The group of books with which we dealt with here, the apocryphal works, is important not only to those interested in the literary creations of the Jewish people during the Second Temple period, but also to those who deal with the aggadic literature of our Sages, and that for three reasons. Firstly — thematically: In the case of many motifs which appeared to have been formulated at the time of our Sages, we find that they existed many years earlier. This, of course, aids us in accurate dating and also eliminates optical illusions, as when it appears that a certain aggadic tradition was created in the 4th, 6th or 8th century C.E., whereas in truth it is far more ancient.

The second reason relates to the different literary types and genres. It appears that the most popular books during the Second Temple era were the ones that retold the Bible stories in different forms (there are those who refer to this genre as "the rewritten Bible"). This includes The Book of Jubilees and The Testaments, The Book of Enoch and The Book of Adam and Eve, as well as other books. This fact is very interesting, because during the era of our Sages this type of work disappeared, and from the 2nd to the 7th or 8th centuries C.E. no books of this type are to be found. The existence of this literary genre before the era of our Sages (and again much after it) brings us to regard the literature of our Sages in a different light.

And the third reason, which is possibly the most important of all, is the fact that many aggadic traditions, which had previously been thought — before we became aware of the apocryphal works — as having been written in the era of our Sages using the technique of the midrash — i.e., by laying special emphasis on a specific textual point and by going into the details of the Biblical text — were not created using these techniques, and had already existed in the literary and cultural eras before our Sages. This requires us to describe (although not always!) the midrashic process not as a creative process which produced new ideas, but as a process whose entire strength consisted of linking existing traditions to the

Biblical text. By dealing with the literature of our Sages while ignoring its underlying foundation, which includes the apocryphal books, we will be seriously hampering our study of the material.

III.

The Jewish-Hellenistic Literature

A contemporary of the apocryphal books — with which the previous chapter dealt — is the Jewish-Hellenistic literature. For our purposes, it will be sufficient if we define it as follows: a group of literary works that were written in Greek by Jews, generally in the familiar literary forms of the Hellenistic culture, the primary purpose being the presentation of Jewish values to the Gentile world in a way dictated primarily by apologetic considerations. This definition attempts to encompass a rather large number of works, some of which we only have in fragmented versions, which were created in the great Jewish-Hellenistic center of Alexandria, in Eretz Israel, and in various Hellenistic colonies, such as in North Africa or Asia Minor, from the 3rd century B.C.E. to the 2nd century C.E. (and there is a certain overlap between these books and the apocryphal works, for some of the latter — such as part of the Books of the Maccabees —were written in literary and cultural circles that were close to, if not identical with, those from whose midst there emerged the Jewish-Hellenistic literature).

If one is permitted to make a generalization about this varied body of literature — and with all the care that must be taken in every generalization — one can state that there are two basic characteristics of Jewish-Hellenistic literature: first — it is a literary and cultural expression of the mighty confrontation between Hellenism and the Semitic culture in general and Jewish culture in particular. The differences between Greek culture and

The World of the Aggadah

Jewish culture are almost unimaginably immense: different religious outlooks, different philosophies, different political and social views (such as the social structure in Greece as opposed to the theocratic culture of Eretz Israel), differences in language (Hebrew and Aramaic on the one hand, Greek on the other) and in their literary (the great epochs of Homer, for example, on the one hand, and the Bible on the other) and cultural traditions (such as their views on sport, sculpture, the extolling of bodily beauty, etc.). This confrontation between the two different cultures created a long string of literary works that wished to merge the two cultures, but the works differ from one another on the question of the relationship between the Hellenistic material and the Jewish material which they use: there are works where the Jewish content predominates, but there are others where the Hellenistic infrastructure is paramount.

The second characteristic of this literature — and it stems to a certain extent from the first — is its clearly apologetic and polemical tone. At first glance there is a contradiction between these two aims, but in practice they complement one another: to be apologetic means to defend oneself, and in our case this meant a clarification of Judaism and its values to the outside and hostile world or to one's weak brothers at home; to be polemical implies involvement in dispute and in attack, a struggle with a foreign culture in which one demonstrates that it is inferior. When the two come together, the two aims give us a literature which fought its battles by a twofold method: by informing, apologizing and explaining on the one hand, and by attacking, mocking and arguing on the other. Both of these approaches were directed to both the outside world (the Gentile world) and internally (to those Jews who dealt with the outside world).

We have enough evidence to assume that already in the ancient Hellenistic world there existed an ample literature that was based on hatred on the Jews, which may be said to be one of the roots of modern-day anti-Semitism. The source of this literature was probably envy but may even have been based on ignorance (for ignorance has always been the primary cause of causeless hatred).

The authors of this literature wished to deal with an ancient and extremely different culture from their own, a culture which they were unable to understand or fathom. In Hellenistic circles, and especially in Alexandria, a number of works were written whose primary purpose was to besmirch, mock and scorn the Jews and Judaism. In these works there were numerous attacks on the rite of circumcision, because this appeared to the authors as barbaric and an affront to the ideal of physical beauty, and the rite was almost considered to be like castration. These circles were also tremendously opposed to the Sabbath, because they could not understand the idea underlying a day of rest and holiness. Instead, they regarded it as a day of idleness, laziness and uncontrolled gluttony. They also regarded the Jews' chaste sex life as peculiar, and they therefore mocked this as well. A very common tradition among the Hellenistic circles described Jewish history as one of lepers: it was because of this dreadful disease that the Israelites were expelled from Egypt, for the Egyptians detested the Israelites and could not stand them. Moses was the leader of this people with this dreaded disease. Another opinion, which also appears in the literature of the ancient Jew-haters, stated that in the Holy of the Holies in the Temple there stood an idol of a golden ass. And there are numerous other examples of this kind. (Incidentally, in order to balance the picture, we should note that the Greek and Roman literature also offer examples of expressions of appreciation for Judaism.)

An interesting fragment of this anti-Jewish literature is to be found in one of the midrashic compilations, *Midrash Ekhah Rabbah*. This midrash was only edited in the 5th century C.E., but contains ancient traditions. R' Abahu of Caesarea (an important city in his days, which was populated by Jews and Greeks) describes how the non-Jews spend their time in their theaters and what they say there about the Jews. As examples, he quotes four passages from anti-Jewish plays, and there is no reason to doubt their historic veracity. Below, I will bring two of them (from *Ekhah Rabbah, Petihta* 17).

In one of these passages, we are given a short dialogue. One of the two choruses on the stage asks the other: "How many years do you wish to live?" The other answers: "As the Sabbath cloak of the Jews." This evidently means that the Jews made a point of not wearing on the Sabbath the clothes they wore during the rest of the week, so as to enhance this holy day and to differentiate it from the rest of the week. Financially, though, there were many people that could not afford to have various sets of clothes. They would therefore set aside separate articles of clothing for the Sabbath, and these would be handed down from one generation to the next. Even if these clothes were eventually full of patches, they were still reserved for the Sabbath. The Gentiles, who did not understand the importance of the Sabbath and the desire to show the difference between it and the other days of the week, used the fact that these clothes were kept for so long a time as a mocking symbol of anything that lasts eternally: one who wishes to live a long life prays that he should live as long as does the Jew's cloak.

And another passage from an anti-Jewish play: A camel enters the theater covered with shrouds, and it looks as if it is in mourning. One chorus asks the other: "Why is this animal mourning?" The other answers: "The Jews observe the sabbatical law [i.e., they allow their land to lie fallow during the seventh, sabbatical year], and they have no vegetables. They therefore ate [the camel's] thorns, and that is why the camel is in mourning." Here we have a case of poking fun at the Jews based on not understanding the commandments, in which the Jews are regarded as competing with and at the same level as the camel. This play even claims that the Jew is responsible for every shortage. This is a well-known anti-Semitic claim, which has been used even in modern times.

It was primarily against such conceptions that the literature which we will be dealing with below, the Jewish-Hellenistic literature, was written. I have chosen to deal here with only three authors, who reflect different forms of dealing with the merger of the Jewish content with Hellenistic content.

The first person we will deal with was the playwright Ezekiel, known as Ezekiel the Poet (in Hebrew usage, he is known as "the

Tragedian"). Ezekiel evidently lived in the major Jewish center of Alexandria in the 2nd century B.C.E., but he may have lived in Qirini or some other cultural center of those days. He wrote a number of plays, using the style of the classic Greek tragedies (hence his Hebrew epithet), and these dealt with Jewish topics. This is thus an example of a merger between the Hellenistic form and Jewish themes. There is no reason to assume that these plays were aimed only at Jews: it is very logical to assume that non-Jews as well came to see them, and thus they understood Judaism in the terms that Ezekiel portrayed it.

Even though Ezekiel wrote a number of plays, we only have sizable extracts of one of these, a play called *Exodus*, much of which was reconstructed by Joshua Gutmann (1890—1963), based on isolated passages and quotes from secondary and tertiary sources. The play deals with Moses, whose special place in the Jewish-Hellenistic literature will yet be dealt with. The play describes the life of Moses: his childhood, his fleeing to Midian, his encounter with God at the burning bush, and the Egyptian plagues. The play ends with a dramatic description of the crossing of the Sea of Reeds and the drowning of the Egyptians. Ezekiel basically follows the Biblical account, but he expands on it and adds many details, new individuals, descriptions of the landscape and dialogues. The play is a tragedy in five acts, as was the typical Greek tragedy of the day. There are never more than two or three individuals on the stage at any given time — and this too was customary at the time. It is possible that there was a chorus there as well, which filled the role assigned to it in the ancient tragedy, expressing its opinion about what was happening and explaining it to the viewer.

Gutmann, who translated the passages of the play into Hebrew, did so in the form customary today for writing scripts. Thus, for example, Ezekiel describes the encounter between Moses and God at the bush as follows:

God's Voice: What is that thing in your hand? Tell me swiftly!

Moses: A staff for those that crawl on four and for people.

God's Voice: Throw it to the ground, hurry away, because it will become a terrible snake.

Moses:	Behold it was thrown ... O Lord, remember Your mercy, so awe-inspiring, so fear-inducing, take pity on me, I tremble at its sight!
God's Voice:	Do not fear, stretch forth your hand and take hold of its tail and it will again become a staff as it was.

Such a description of the events may appear to us to be somewhat naive, but one should see it primarily from the viewpoint of the non-Jew of the 2nd century B.C.E. who went to the theater, and in light of the limitations imposed by the facilities available to the playwrights of the time.

Ezekiel includes in the play, in addition to Moses, God's voice, Jethro, Zipporah, and other individuals, including one named Chum, who has but one line in the fragments of the play we have, but it is a line which is thought-provoking. It appears that Chum and Zipporah are on the stage, and he says to her: "You, Zipporah, have to tell me all about this," and she answers, "My father gave me to this foreigner as a wife." One can surmise that Zipporah had been engaged to Chum, until the "foreigner," Moses, arrived, and by his arrival, we learn, brought about a rift between Zipporah and Chum, and the two lines I quoted may be the scene in which the two part. The Jewish authors, as we will yet see, loved love stories among their heroes, and the adding of this man named Chum to the Biblical story furthered this aim.

In another passage in the play, we find a dialogue between Moses and Reu'el (another name for Jethro, Moses' father-in-law). Moses tells his father-in-law of a dream that he had dreamed, something of which there is no hint in the Bible, and thus he says:

At the peak of Mount Sinai a very tall throne that reached to the heavens was revealed to me, and upon it sat some type of exalted man, with a crown on his head and a very large scepter in his left hand. With his right hand he motioned to me, and I stood before the throne. He then handed me the crown and told me to sit on the great throne. He handed me the royal crown while he himself moved away from the throne. I looked down upon the entire earth round about, as well as at what is beneath the world and above the heavens, and the constellations of stars fell upon their knees, and I counted all of them ... After I awoke, I was overcome with fear.

Jethro, Moses' father-in-law, interprets the dream for him:

My friend, God has shown you favor in your dream ... because you will indeed establish a great monarchical throne, and you yourself will lead mortals and will head them. As to seeing the earth and all in it and what is below it and above God's skies, the meaning is that you will see the present and what came before and what will yet come to be.

In the dream and its interpretation, Moses is portrayed in a very positive light, as a superior being, almost Divine, a prophet, a king, and of great power. This, of course, was very much in keeping with the aim of the Jewish-Hellenistic authors, which was to extol and exalt the heroes of the Jewish people, and especially Moses, whom the anti-Jewish literature had portrayed as the leader of a band of lepers.

Ezekiel the Poet is thus a good example of the integration of a Greek form, the tragedy, and Jewish topics, as a portrait of Moses and his history.

A contemporary of Ezekiel, who also belonged to the group of Jewish-Hellenistic writers, was an author named Artapanus, a historiographer who evidently lived in Alexandria in the 2nd century B.C.E. His works showed a blend of Hellenistic themes and Jewish history, and he devoted a great deal of attention — in accordance with the Jewish-Hellenistic tradition in general — to Moses, whom he depicted, no more and no less, along lines borrowed from the description of an ancient Egyptian-Hellenistic god, Hermes-Thoth. The legends told by various ancient pagan Egyptian and Hellenistic authors about that god are told by Artapanus about Moses: It was he who invented writing and culture, he who founded technology, and he who established political government. Almost everything that the Egyptian-Hellenistic world attributed to its gods, Artapanus attributes —out of clearly apologetic motives — to Moses.

Below is an example of one of the interesting stories that the author tells about Moses:

> The Egyptian king had a daughter named Maris, and he married her off to a certain man ... As she was barren, she took for herself one of the sons of the Israelites and called him Moses ... When he grew up, he taught people many useful things. He invented ships and machines to lay rocks, the Egyptian weaponry and the devices used for watering, as well as philosophy ... He divided the country into thirty-six regions, and for each region he assigned one of his gods to be served ... As a result, Moses was beloved by the masses, and was respected by the priests with the respect given to God. He was known as Hermes.

We see how the author identifies Moses completely with the foreign god, and how he attributes to him the formulation of civilization in general, as if telling his readers that everything good that they possess stems from a Jewish source.

And he continues:

> [The Egyptian king] envied him [i.e., Moses], and sought an acceptable excuse to kill him. And as in those days the Ethiopians were fighting Egypt, it occurred to [the king] that this was a good time to send Moses against them as the commanding officer, at the head of the army. He placed a vast throng of farmers at his disposal, with the assumption that he would be killed easily by the enemy because of the weakness of his soldiers. Moses then went to the region known as Hermopolis [i.e., the city of Hermes], with a hundred thousand soldiers at his disposal, and that was where he established his camp ... The war lasted ten years. Moses' people founded a city in that place ... and in that city they sanctified the owl, because it destroys those animals which cause damage to man ... The Ethiopians too, even though they were enemies, loved Moses so much that they learned from him to circumcise their sons.

Even a fast and cursory reading of the words indicates the heroic figure of a Jewish military commander in service of Egypt, an officer who is depicted along lines which were certainly taken from a Hellenistic-Egyptian tradition dealing with one of their gods: the victory over the Ethiopians, who were the Egyptians' neighbors to the south, the building of a city named after the god, the sanctification of living creatures, etc. Artapanus thus blends Hellenistic literary motifs of an almost mythological character with Jewish traditions (on Moses, his links with the Egyptian king, etc.), and in this he illustrates clearly the Jewish-Hellenistic cultural mix that characterized the Jews of Alexandria in the last two centuries B.C.E.

The third in this collection of authors, and possibly one of the most important, is Philo the Alexandrian, whose name tells us where he lived. He was born in 20 B.C.E. and died at about the age of 70. He was the member of a distinguished Jewish family that was proud of its religion. Philo was primarily a philosopher, and his works reveal to us the way in which the Hellenistic methods of thought were mixed with the traditional Jewish materials. From this point of view, Philo, Ezekiel and Artapanus — each in his own way — represent three possible ways of blending Judaism and Hellenism: Jewish content shaped into a Hellenistic form; Jewish motifs mixed with Hellenistic; and Jewish subject matter which passes through a new system of thought.

Philo wrote a great number of works in Greek (it is doubtful whether he read Hebrew; it appears that he knew the Bible from the Greek translation), and they can generally be divided into three groups: a) A group which includes allegorical discussions about the Holy Scriptures. Philo retells Biblical stories, while understanding them as allegories related to other topics (as we will illustrate below). b. Another type of writing is the biographies of the forefathers of the Jewish people (Abraham, Moses, Joseph), in which the author combines the account as told in the Torah with his unique religious and philosophical views. c. The third type includes questions and answers on the books of Genesis and Exodus, in which Philo asks questions on the Bible according to the sequence in the text, and answers them while adding his own views on the Biblical stories and laws.

Those scholars who have dealt with Philo's writings claim that there is no great philosophical innovation in his words. He relies primarily on the writings of Plato, and his thought is based primarily on a clear merger in his writings between Greek philosophy and Jewish tradition. He wished to tell both his fellow-Jews and his foreign readers that in reality there is an overlap between the Torah and Greek philosophy, and there is no significant difference between the two. Thus *the merger* of the two methods of thought is Philo's innovation, and not necessarily the ideas which he merges together. And indeed, one of the Fathers of the Church, Jerome (who will yet be mentioned in the discussion on Christianity) said, in speaking of Plato and Philo: "One of the two: Either Plato is Philoizing or Philo is Platoizing," i.e., the two philosophers are so close in thought that it is difficult for one who does not know the chronological order of the two to know who is the original and who the copy.

Philo, as we noted, did not read Hebrew, but his writings reflect a large number of Jewish traditions, which he had evidently absorbed while listening in the synagogue to various *darshanim* or to those who translated the Bible into Greek. From this point of view, Philo — as well as Ezekiel, Artapanus or the apocryphal works — serves as an external source for dating aggadic traditions with which we are familiar from the rabbinic literature. Thus, for example, Philo states that a slave who does not wish to be freed must have his ear pierced, because he committed a sin with this organ of his body, and that is exactly what our Sages said hundreds of years later:

> Why should the ear be more worthy of being pierced than all the other organs? Because it heard from Mount Sinai, "For unto Me the Children of Israel are servants" ... and yet it removed from itself the Yoke of Heaven [by becoming enslaved to a mortal] ... let the ear come and be pierced for not having obeyed what it heard (*Tosefta Bava Kama* 7b).

Philo, too, like the Midrash, tells us, for example, that Noah was only righteous in comparison to his generation; that Cain brought a sacrifice from his inferior crops rather than from the best; that Adam was born androgynous (i.e., half male and half female) — and these motifs appear in the literature of our Sages only hundreds of years after Philo.

Below is a single example, a relatively simple one, as to what Philo does with Bible stories. In his work on the life of Joseph, he tells of the latter's dreams, and these are his words about the second dream, that of the sun, the moon and the stars:

> [Joseph] brought his brothers word of another dream, more amazing than the first ... In his dream, behold the sun and the moon and eleven stars came and bowed down to him. His father was amazed, and kept the matter locked up in his heart, waiting to see what would happen, but he scolded his son ... and said: Will we surely come — I and your mother and your brothers — to bow down to you to the ground? Your father — that is the sun in your dream. Your mother is the moon, and the eleven stars — your brothers. Do not take this seriously, forget the dream and do not think of it.

Until this point, Philo gives the reader, in a more or less accurate form, the Biblical story, but afterwards he gives expression to his view of the events: "because it is shameful for a person to seek to rule over his relatives. And I believe that all those who are concerned about equality and about proper relationships think as I do." Philo then goes on to mention that Jacob was afraid that if all the brothers lived together it would bring about quarrels and strife between them, and "therefore he sent them to graze the sheep, while he left him [i.e., Joseph] at home" (and this tradition — that Jacob sent his sons with the sheep in order to separate them from Joseph, so that they would not quarrel among themselves, is one that I have not found in any other source). Again, Philo adds his own philosophic view: "He [Jacob] certainly knew that time heals the passions and illnesses of the soul, and it is it which melts distress, soothes anger and assuages wrath, because time soothes all."

So far, we have seen a text which retells the Biblical story, while expanding on it with various aggadic traditions and weaving into it different social, religious and philosophical values of Philo. Thus, immediately afterwards, Philo continues and adds:

> It is proper and pleasing to interpret the hidden meaning (of the Bible) after giving its simple meaning, for almost the entire Torah, or at least the majority of the Torah, speaks allegorically.

45

From that point on, he tells his readers the story of Joseph and his brothers as a complex web of allegories, where Joseph is depicted as a symbol of proper government. Thus, for example, Philo explains the coat of many colors that Joseph received from his father as symbolizing political life, which is "striped ... and varied as a mosaic. It includes an infinite amount of exchanges and substitutions that are caused by individuals, events and circumstances," for no day resembles another, nor one minute another. Furthermore, the sale of Joseph into slavery is but a symbol of the idea that the leader is the servant of the people: "For the speaker or preacher who ascends to the dais — like slaves who are put up for sale — is transformed from a free man to a slave, and in spite of all the honors that he thinks he will accrue, he is led captive by tens of thousands of masters." Philo continues to imbue many details of the story of Joseph and his brothers with other meanings, which transform them into an allegory whose concern — in this case — is the proper way that the true leader must lead his nation.

In addition to the above three — Ezekiel, Artapanus and Philo — there were also many other authors in the Jewish-Hellenistic society, some of whose writings were not preserved. The most important of all of these as far as we are concerned is Joseph ben Mattathias (Josephus), to whom the following chapter will be devoted. While dealing with Josephus, we will again explain the importance of the Jewish-Hellenistic literature in the proper and complete understanding of the aggadic literature of our Sages.

IV.

Josephus

We must devote a separate discussion to the most important and prominent individual among the Jewish-Hellenistic authors with whom we dealt in the previous chapter, namely Joseph ben Mattathias, or, as he is generally known, Josephus Flavius. Josephus was born in Jerusalem in 37 C.E. and died in Rome in about 100 C.E. His life was tortuous and complex, as we learn from his writings.

Josephus was a member of the priestly clan, a public figure in Jerusalem, who left on a political mission to Rome in the year 64 C.E. in order to negotiate the release of captives. His confrontation with mighty Rome and its culture influenced him greatly. He was seized by the idea of Rome, became a supporter of the empire, and from that time on the course of his life changed almost entirely. Josephus returned to Eretz Israel and served as a commander in the Galilee during the Great Revolt, the same revolt which brought about the destruction of the Second Temple. During the revolt, as much as we are able to believe Josephus himself, he attempted to maintain a relatively moderate position and was constantly at odds with the zealots, who demanded a bolder and more forceful military effort.

In the end — and this is the major, but also the most controversial point regarding his life history — Josephus found himself in the Roman camp. Did he betray his brothers when he joined their enemies? That is the major question, but there is no clear answer to it, because on this issue the only evidence we have is that of Josephus himself, and it is natural that he did not dwell on this at too great a length. In any event, at that time Josephus befriended a Roman who would later be the emperor, Vespasian, and his son Titus. According to Josephus, the emperor befriended him because he, Josephus, had predicted that Vespasian would eventually be the ruler of Rome.

Josephus was forced to witness the destruction of Eretz Israel and the fall of the Temple. According to him, he tried to persuade those under siege in Jerusalem to submit and thereby to prevent a bloodbath, but they refused to listen to him. After Jerusalem fell and the Temple was burned down (and according to Josephus this was not done at Titus' orders!), Josephus moved to Rome, became a Roman citizen and lived in that city under the patronage of the emperor, while he devoted his remaining days to writing his major work.

Josephus' literary output consists of four works, the fourth of which will occupy us more than the others, but we will review all of them to obtain a comprehensive picture. As they are part of the Jewish-Hellenistic literature, they were, of course, written in Greek, and were meant first and foremost for the non-Jewish reader.

One famous work is *The Jewish War*, a book which describes the sequence of events that brought about the revolt and the destruction. In truth, this is the major source we have of that era, and historians are divided over the question whether one can rely on Josephus' account or not. It is true that in the end Josephus states: "As to the style, the reader will offer his own judgment, but regarding the veracity, I promise and am not afraid to state that that was all that I aimed at in these words," but there are many who believe that Josephus' end as a Roman citizen and one under the patronage of the emperor influenced his view of the way he describes the events. There are also striking differences between Josephus' statements in this work and his statements in other works, and this fact too, of course, makes it difficult to accept all his words as unquestionable truth.

Another of his works, which clearly belongs to the Jewish-

Hellenistic body of literature as we described it in the previous chapter, is named *Against Apion*. This is a polemical work against an author named Apion, who had written very negatively about Judaism. In this work Josephus is shown to be a proud Jew, who fights his people's battle and attempts in various ways to persuade the reader that Apion is wrong. Among others, for example, he attacks the statement — which appears time and again in many Hellenistic works — that the Jewish people had been expelled from Egypt in disgrace because they had all been lepers, and that they had been led by the chief of the lepers — Moses. This is the way Josephus deals with this claim:

> This man [i.e., Moses] had no blemish in his skin, as can be seen from what he himself said, for he forbade all lepers to live in the city ... and he decreed that all that touched their flesh would be ritually impure ... Even when [a leper's] blemish was healed, he decreed the leper had to undergo many purifications ... and if the legislator [= Moses] had suffered this disease, it would have been proper for him to favor those people who suffered the same disease as he, and to be merciful to them.

From this, Josephus deduces that it was impossible for Moses to have been a leper. Using similar methods, he proceeds to demolish other anti-Jewish claims to be found in the literature of the era.

Another work of Josephus, with which we have already dealt without mentioning it by name, is his autobiography, *The Life of Josephus*, and that is the major source from which we learn about his life. The work begins with a declaration which is hardly a model of modesty: "I am not a nameless son, but a descendant [on my father's side] of an ancient priestly family ... On my mother's side, I am of royal stock, because she was of the Hasmonean family." Later, Josephus describes his youth ("I did well in my studies and was considered to be exceptional"), his departure for Rome and his involvement in communal matters. He also tells of the war in which the Temple was destroyed (and here we are faced by difficult questions, because he sometimes contradicts what he wrote in *The Jewish War*), and even describes his life in Rome, his wives and his children. According to him, he married four women and had a total of five children by them.

The three works of Josephus which we have mentioned until now in brief, are especially important to anyone dealing with the history of the Jewish people and the history of the Jewish-Gentile debate of those days. His fourth work, with which we will deal from now on, is the most significant in terms of the topic at hand. This was possibly Josephus' life work, the book entitled *The Antiquities of the Jews*. It contains twenty parts and is a detailed description of the history of the world and of the Jewish people from the Creation to the war in which the Temple was destroyed. In many ways this work may be regarded as an introduction to *The Jewish War*, a work that Josephus had written earlier. *The Antiquities of the Jews* was written in Rome, between approximately 73 — 93 C.E., i.e., over a period of about twenty years, and its aim — as that of all of the Jewish-Hellenistic literature — was to enlighten the Gentiles and to have them understand the nature of Judaism and its values, for we have already seen that at the time there was abysmal ignorance in the non-Jewish world about Judaism, accompanied by stereotypes that were nurtured by various anti-Jewish works.

As far as we are concerned, the most important are the first eleven parts of *The Antiquities*, Books I — XI, which deal with the Biblical era and retell everything mentioned in the Bible about the events from the creation of the world until Esther's time. Josephus was a faithful disciple of his teachers, the Jerusalem scholars of the 1st century C.E., for (as he writes in his autobiography) he studied Torah in Jerusalem, was considered to be a prodigy, and a glowing future was predicted for him. Much of what he heard in the study halls in Jerusalem or in other contexts (such as lectures in the synagogues) he put into his books. On the other hand, as we mentioned, Josephus was writing for the non-Jewish reader, and many of the characteristic traits of Jewish-Hellenistic literature are to be found in his works as well. Thus we have an interesting combination of traditions familiar to us at a later time in the literature of our Sages, and motifs and ways of expression known to us from the general Hellenistic literature, which Josephus attempted to blend together and to form something new.

Josephus' use of the Biblical stories was selective, and he omitted from his works whatever he found unpalatable or that he felt his potential readers might find distasteful. Thus, for example, *The Antiquities of the Jews* carries no reference to the story of the Golden Calf, a story which portrays the Jewish people in a poor light, as a nation of sinners who betrayed their religion; or the story of Moses killing the Egyptian. It was impossible for Josephus to portray the leader of the Jewish people and the founder of its religion as a hot-tempered murderer. (In order to justify Moses' leaving Egypt for Midian, he therefore had to find another explanation.) And of course he did not mention Miriam's leprosy, for every hint, even the most veiled, to the existence of this dreadful and fearful disease among the heads of the Jewish people would be greeted with exultation by the Jew-haters of the time.

Josephus organizes his work, based on the Hellenistic literary tradition, about various central figures (such as Abraham, Jacob or Joseph), and the description of these individuals and of their deeds is often in keeping with the literary rules of the Hellenistic world. This is expressed first and foremost in the many long and complex speeches that Josephus attributes to the individuals, in the best tradition of Greek rhetoric. He also includes — and this too was common in Hellenistic literature —love stories. Whatever is not mentioned in the Bible, or is merely alluded to or hinted at, is expanded upon by Josephus. Thus, for example, he describes a romance between Joseph and Potiphar's wife, or he has a wonderful story, which we will deal with immediately, of Moses' marriage to the woman of Cush. Josephus also describes at length the emotional feelings of the characters involved, and there is a certain emphasis on the psychological aspect of the events, while making the story palatable to the Hellenistic reader. What is very interesting is how Josephus deals with miracles: his faith as a Jew requires him to accept them literally, but his rationalist view — and his fear of what his readers might say — appears to be in contradiction to this faith, and there are thus numerous occasions when we find an attempt at rationalizing the miracle. Where this is impossible, though, he has no hesitation in stating that "about these matters" [in this case he is referring to God's revelation on Mount Sinai], each of my readers may think as he wishes, but I must tell it as it is written in the Holy Scriptures."

Whatever has been said until now I would like to illustrate with two somewhat detailed examples. The first example is taken from Josephus' account of Moses' war against the people of Cush and his marriage to a woman of Cush. We have already hinted at this story (in the previous chapter), when we dealt with the Jewish-Hellenistic historian Artapanus, who describes Moses as the commander of Pharaoh's army who went out to fight the people of Cush. But Josephus — who repeats this story (and it is possible that he knew it in whole or in part from the writings of Artapanus) — brings it in greatly expanded form. And this is what he writes (in *The Antiquities*):

> The people of Cush, the neighbors of the Egyptians, invaded their land and took and carried away their property ... They spread throughout the entire land, and once they had tasted of its riches they refused to give it up ... The Egyptians were in great distress, and they turned to words of prophecy and witchcraft. When God advised them to take the Hebrews as allies, the king ordered his daughter [Moses' adopted mother] to send Moses to him, so as to be the commander of the army. She gave him [to her father] after he had sworn to her that no harm would befall him ... And Moses accepted the position gladly, according to the request of Thermouthis [according to Josephus, that was his Egyptian "mother's" name] and the king ... Moses went and led the army, before their enemies knew that he had left, and he took his troops not alongside the river [as had been customary in previous military campaigns], but along the dry land. Here he gave a wonderful sign of his brilliance. That land is difficult to walk on because of the many snakes which it breeds ... And Moses invented a marvelous way to provide security for his army ... He prepared reed baskets which resembled arks and filled them with owls. This creature is the

most dreaded enemy of snakes, and they flee when the owls attack them ... And in this way he made his march and arrived at the people of Cush, who did not expect him at all, and he attacked them and vanquished them in battle... He killed many among them ... Finally, [the people of Cush] were repulsed to Sheba, which was the capital city of Cush, and were besieged. The place could not be conquered except with difficulty, because the Nile surrounds it, and other rivers also make it a difficult place for battle for those wishing to cross the current ... And as Moses unwillingly waited while his troops were inactive ... the following event occurred: The king of the people of Cush had a daughter, whose name was Tharbis. She saw Moses as he led his troops close to the wall and fought bravely, and she was amazed at the brilliance of his plans. She assumed that it was he who had brought Egypt all its success ... She became very enamored of him. When this feeling overpowered her, she sent her trusty servants to speak to him of marriage. He agreed to talk provided that the city be surrendered. They then made a pact with an oath, that he would truthfully marry the woman and would not violate the contract after conquering the city. The talk and the act came one after the other, and Moses thanked God. After punishing the people of Cush and making a marriage pact, he brought the Egyptians back to their land.

Thus we have before us a love story between Moses and the daughter of the king of Cush, where she marries Moses in return for her treachery to her people and her surrendering the city. This story is evidently modelled on various Hellenistic stories, on the woman who is a traitor to her own city because of her love for an enemy military commander. And indeed Avraham Shalit, who, among others, translated the above passage of Josephus into Hebrew, brings parallels to this story in a number of Greek stories based on a similar type of plot. According to Shalit, various Jewish-Hellenistic circles (or possibly Josephus himself) combined a foreign story with the revered Biblical character of Moses (and compare the puzzling verse in Num. 12:1). By doing so, they created something new, which the non-Jewish reader — and we should stress again that *The*

Antiquities of the Jews was written primarily for this reader — could understand and enjoy, and could therefore regard Moses in a different light from that portrayed in the anti-Jewish literature of the era. (Incidentally, we may note that this story was kept alive in the traditional Jewish literature, and appears in a greatly expanded form in *Sefer ha-Yashar*, one of the most popular works of the Jewish people in the Middle Ages.)

Another, more complex example, but no less important for our topic, is Josephus' story of the birth of Moses:

Amram, one of the most prominent Hebrews, was in fear for his nation [because of Pharaoh's decree to kill all male infants], for the entire nation might be wiped out for lack of a young generation ... And he was at a loss as to what to do, for his wife was pregnant ... He prayed to God and pleaded that He grant mercy to His creatures ... and that He redeem them from their suffering ... God took mercy upon him and accepted his plea, appearing to him in a dream and persuading him not to give up hope of the future ... [and at this point there is a long speech, according to the Jewish-Hellenistic tradition, in which God reveals to Amram the future, and even tells him of the birth of Moses and of his fate and his assignment] ... These things were revealed to Amram in a dream ... And the birth by the woman [Jochebed] added faith regarding that which they had been heralded by God, for she disappeared from the eyes of the guards because of the mildness of her birth pangs and because they did not cause her severe pain. For three months she hid the child ... [and then] they decided to entrust to God his rescue [and here Josephus tells us about Moses who was cast into the river and how he was saved by the daughter of the king, Thermouthis] ... When Moses was three years old, God made him remarkably tall, and no man who had a sense of beauty could but be amazed at Moses' handsomeness from the instant he saw him. And many who happened by chance to meet him .. were attracted by the appearance of the child and would leave their work to gaze at him ... Once Thermouthis took Moses to her father and showed him to him ... She placed the child in her father's arms. The latter took him and adopted him lovingly, placing the crown on his head so as to give his daughter pleasure. Moses then took the crown and threw it to the ground in what might appear but a childish prank, and stamped upon it with his foot. This was regarded as an omen of troubles that would befall the monarchy. When the astrologer who had predicted in advance that a child would be born who would bring the Egyptian monarchy down saw this, he arose to kill him ... Thermouthis, though, interceded and saved the child from his hands.

This story is especially interesting if we do not forget the date when it was written: many years before our Sages' works were committed to writing. And yet we find that many of the motifs mentioned by Josephus appear much later in the Midrash and the Talmud, quoted in the names of sages who lived hundreds of years after him, in the 4th and 5th centuries C.E. From this point of view, Josephus' writings also serve as a chronological starting point which aids us in dating with greater accuracy traditions known to us from the literature of our Sages. Thus, for example, similar to the statement by Josephus that Amram was one of the most prominent of the Hebrews, we find in the Babylonian Talmud (*Sotah* 12a) that Amram was "the greatest man of his generation." The same is true about Josephus' statement regarding the mild birth pains suffered by Jochebed. Here too the Babylonian Talmud (*ibid.*) states, this time quoting R' Judah b. Zavina, that "the birth was painless."

And on this last point we have a fascinating question. R' Judah, when he states that Jochebed's birth was painless, deduces this by utilizing one of the methods of interpretation used in the Midrash, i.e., by examining in a unique fashion the exact wording of the Biblical text. In the Torah account we are told in regard to Moses' mother that "she conceived ... and she bore a son," and the Midrash asks: "Why does it state that 'she conceived'?" After all, even without the statement, wouldn't we know that before a woman can give birth she must first conceive? And as the authors of the Midrash believe that there is not a single superfluous word in the Torah, they are forced to interpret "she conceived" in a way that

55

will justify its appearance in the verse. The Midrash therefore states that "she conceived" was brought here to teach us something that we would not know without it — or, in other words: the statement "she conceived," which appears to be superfluous, is not meant to teach us anything in itself, but rather to teach us about the following statement, that "she bore a son." The Midrash continues: Just as the conception was without pain, so too was the birth. Thus the *darshan* "proves," as it were, his statement that Jochebed gave birth painlessly, using an accepted method of interpretation of the Midrash (known as *hekesh* —"juxtaposition"). Yet, here we find that the painless birth was already known to Josephus hundreds of years before R' Judah. This fact forces us to reexamine the question of the deduction of aggadic traditions from the Biblical verses by means of one of the methods of the Midrash, for we now are faced with one of two possibilities — either this method of deduction from the text was already known to Josephus (even though he never mentioned it specifically), and this would mean that the method is more ancient than thought previously, or that R' Judah is not telling us anything new, and is merely linking this ancient tradition to the Biblical verse. Whichever of the two possibilities we choose is of great importance regarding the history of the Midrashic methods.

In conclusion, we will make a further brief comment about the story that Josephus brings about Moses, who takes Pharaoh's crown from his head and throws it to the ground. This story occurs again in Hebrew literature in a much later era, evidently only in the 9th or 10th century C.E., but here it is expanded on greatly. According to our literature (see, for example, *Midrash Shemot Rabbah* 1:26), after one of Pharaoh's astrologers (it is customary to identify him with Balaam) attempts to kill Moses for having thrown the crown to the ground, another astrologer intervenes (according to a number of traditions this being Jethro) and suggests that Moses be put to the test. A burning coal and a gold coin are to be placed before him, and all are to see what he will pick up, or, as the Midrash puts it: "If he stretches forth his hand to the gold, it shows he is wise and he is to be killed, and if he stretches forth his hand to the coal, he is not wise and he does not deserve the death penalty." Those present agree to the test, and a glowing coal and a gold coin are brought. Moses reaches for the gold, but an angel pushes his hand from the gold to the coal. When Moses touches the coal, his hand is burned, and in his confusion (or in order to soothe the pain of the burn) he puts his fingers in his mouth, and that is how Moses becomes, as the Torah testifies about him elsewhere, a stammerer.

This story only appears in the Hebrew literature of a late period, but one who reads it carefully will feel that it is very foreign to the common viewpoints and the methods of expression in our ancient literature. First of all, we should note the stress on Moses' physical beauty; our sources do not lay great stress on such descriptions. Another point which is not in keeping with the spirit of Judaism is the test: can one kill a person on the basis of such a test? In addition, can a small child (and Moses was three or four years old at the time) be considered guilty that he should deserve the death penalty, even if he did what he did deliberately? I would therefore venture to say that the story which we read in *Shemot Rabbah* was born outside the circles which created the literature of our Sages, and it may well be an ancient Jewish-Hellenistic story. This would appear logical not only in terms of its content or the fact that there are allusions to it in Josephus, but also because one is able to bring proof from the ancient Greek literature to the existence of similar motifs. Thus we find the following in a Greek tale of the 2nd century B.C.E.: a child steals a gold leaf from the wreath of the god Artemis. In order to know whether the child did this deliberately, he is put to a test. Toys and a gold leaf are placed before him, and when he touches the gold leaf he is sentenced to death. In this Greek tale, we are missing the happy ending, unlike the Hebrew story, but the resemblance in motifs between the two still remains.

From all this we can hypothesize that in this case as well Josephus serves as one of the mediators in the transfer of motifs from the Greek literature to our literature (and, as mentioned earlier, we made the same comment regarding Moses' marriage to the daughter of the king of Cush). It is true that in Josephus' story, as we have it, there is no element of a test between the coal and the gold and only the first part of the story is brought, with the description of Moses' beauty and his grabbing of the crown, but the general nature of the story and its Greek parallel can help us to hypothesize that Josephus, for reasons known to him, took only part of the foreign story which he knew, whereas the full Jewish-Hellenistic tradition continued to exist in various circles, and thus the story only appeared in full in written form at a later time.

It is difficult to overstate the contribution of Josephus to our knowledge of the ancient aggadah. His works are one of the main tools available to the scholar to date aggadic traditions and to discuss their origin and history. All this, of course, is in addition to his great contribution to the study of the history of his time and the study of the beliefs and opinions prevalent among the groups among whom he lived.

V.

The Writings of the Dead Sea Sect

About forty years ago, a real revolution took place in the study of ancient Jewish literature and the history of the Jewish people at the end of the Second Temple era. This revolution was brought about by the publication of a number of writings known by various names: The Dead Sea Sect Scrolls, The Qumran Scrolls, The Judean Desert Scrolls, etc.

It would appear that a small group of Jews separated from the Jewish people some time toward the end of the Second Temple era —evidently during the Hasmonean era — for reasons which we have been unable to fathom fully. They moved to the Judean Desert, in the northern Dead Sea area, and lived there in caves, while devising a special life style and maintaining a fully communal life in groups which were arranged hierarchically. The members of the sect were required to offer full obedience to their leaders; they had stringent rules of behavior, and those who violated the sect's rules were liable to be punished severely, including banishment from the sect. On the other hand, they were scrupulous in the observance of commandments such as prayer and ritual purity, and gave pride of place to the priests in their ranks. They had their own yearly calendar, and they evidently celebrated their own unique festivals.

The founder of the sect, whose name is unknown to us, is referred to in the sect's writings as "the Teacher of Righteousness." One can but surmise that he was a priest who had abandoned — or had possibly been deposed or banished from — the Temple in Jerusalem, for some reason or another. He took a number of his followers with him to the desert and there he preached a new way of life, one which was "anti-establishment," which regarded itself as fighting for the just cause against "the evil priest" or "the evil kingdom," terms evidently referring to the priests in Jerusalem, the kings of the Hasmonean dynasty, and the leaders of the nation in general. The "Teacher of Righteousness" was associated with various elements of messianism, and it is possible that the sect regarded him, after his death, as the messiah who is to come and bring about redemption to the world.

The members of the Dead Sea Sect devised their own way of thought. They believed in predestination: all events in man's life, for better or worse, are determined before he is born, and there is no way to escape the fate decreed upon the individual. As a result, all of mankind is divided up into two groups: the larger group of the sinners, people whose deeds are evil and imperfect, "The Sons of Darkness"; and the small group of "the Sons of Light," who belonged to the sect, and who were the only ones to whom the proper life style was revealed. The latter sat and waited until "the Kingdom of Belial" passed from the earth and the light of redemption would shine forth. Meanwhile, they lived ascetically and cloistered from the world, while engaging in physical work, observing the commandments in ritual purity, studying the Torah and prayer. The sect had been chosen to carry on its shoulders the yoke of the present, which included in itself the promise of the future redemption. When the Day of Judgment would come, the day of retribution at the End of Days, only the members of the sect would be saved, and then a new era — a better one — would begin.

There are those who identify the Dead Sea Sect with the Essenes mentioned by Josephus, but not all scholars agree with this identification. In any event, the sect existed from approximately the Hasmonean era until close to the destruction of the Second Temple, when the Roman might descended equally upon all the inhabitants of the land. One should also note the link that has been revealed between the life style of the members of the sect and ancient Christianity. In both cases they were sects which had left Judaism;

in both cases great stress was paid on baptism and on going down to the wilderness, and both had the same sense of an ancient fate which man cannot escape. One should thus regard the Dead Sea Sect and ancient Christianity as similar phenomena of expressions of dissatisfaction with Judaism, as it had been shaped at the end of the Second Temple era.

Whoever the sect might have been, it was because of the dry climate in the Dead Sea area that we have in our possession a goodly number of manuscripts which had been hidden by members of the sect in various hiding places, and these are of the greatest importance for the topic with which we are dealing.

The manuscripts that were discovered in the areas where the members of the sect resided include, first and foremost, passages from the Bible (such as the Book of Isaiah), whose importance is immense for those who wish to study the text of the Bible and its history, for here for the first time we find a Biblical text exactly as it existed at the time of Alexander Yannai or Hillel the Elder. The Bible which we have, as is known, is only based on a manuscript of the beginning of the Middle Ages, and now the scrolls come and show us clearly — without having to resort to educated guesses — how the Bible appeared in their times, about 800 years before the above-mentioned Bible manuscripts. The differences between the Biblical text in the scrolls and that in our possession are of great significance (and not only in terms of spelling), but they are not pertinent to us here.

One of the works of the Dead Sea Sect is known as The Community Rule. What it is, is a collection of regulations of the sect which give us information on its rules, on the *halakhah* which it observed and on its social structure. Thus, for example, we find that the sect had a leader for every ten men, he being "the expounder of the Torah," who fulfilled literally the verse (Josh. 1:8), "You shall meditate in it day and night." From this work we also learn about the sect's daily life and of its manner of existence.

A work of greater importance to our topic is that known as the Thanksgiving Hymns. This work resembles the Book of Psalms to a certain extent in that it contains poetic texts which are religious hymns. Most of the hymns begin with the phrase, "I thank You, O Lord," and hence the name of the entire work. This work teaches us much, not only about the language spoken in Eretz Israel in those days, but also about the religious views of the sect — for it deals with such topics as belief in God, faith in Him, sin, reward and punishment, the attitude to money, etc. It is also of great value in research on Jewish prayer in general, for our prayer book only attained its present form toward the end of the era of our Sages (and especially at the time of the *Geonim*), and without the Thanksgiving Hymns we would be groping in the dark about the phraseology and the expressions used in prayer in the Second Temple era.

Below is an example of one of the psalms:

Blessed are You O Lord, God of mercy and great in lovingkindness

For You have made known Your wisdom to me / To tell Your marvelous deeds

And not to remain silent by day or night

And to give praise aloud with cymbal and drum

For I long for Your favor / For Your great good and Your abundant forgiveness

And I will constantly hope for Your mercy / For I rely on Your truth. (Thanksgiving Hymns 19 in Hebrew edition; 16 in English edition by G. Vermes)

These words remind us of similar motifs in the Book of Psalms, but also of elements in Jewish prayer later than the Bible, such as the phrase, "Blessed are You," which has been accepted in the standard Jewish liturgy as the introduction to blessings (such as "Blessed are You ... Creator of the fruit of the vine"), or those sentences beginning with the word "For," whose aim is to give the reason why the person is blessing God (such as "for You hear the prayer of each mouth," and so on).

Below is another example from the Thanksgiving hymns. Here too one should pay attention to the content of the verses:

Blessed are You God of mercy and compassion

In Your great good and abundant truth / And the multitude of Your favors in all Your deeds

62

Rejoice the soul of Your servant in Your truth / And purify me in Your righteousness

As I have longed for Your good / and will hope for Your compassion.

(Thanksgiving Hymns 21 in Hebrew edition; 18 in English edition)

One of the very interesting works of the sect is The War of the Sons of Light with the Sons of Darkness. It describes an imaginary war in the eschatological future, a war which will last for forty years, between the powers of light, namely the members of the sect and their supporters, and the powers of darkness, the sons of darkness and the supporters of the kingdom of Belial. The scroll describes at length the mustering of the men into the army and the organization of the forces, the weapons that will be used in the war and the progression of the war, and the praises or thanks that they will recite at every stage. The scroll even gives the names of the angels who will help the Sons of Light to achieve their final victory.

This work — and we are not aware of any similar works in the ancient world — gives us added information about the military strategies of those days and about the question of the belief in angels among various groups within the Jewish people. One should realize that the members of the sect depicted for themselves a great world of angels, who direct man's activities and act at his side, and the scroll even gives us many names of the heavenly hosts (Uriel, Sariel, and others). We will yet have reason to mention that the world of the angels in the literature of our Sages is pale and insipid in comparison to the one depicted in the scrolls, or in the mystic literature with which we will deal in the coming chapter.

In addition to these three works — the Thanksgiving Hymns, the Community Rule and the War of the Sons of Light with the Sons of Darkness — we also have a number of other writings of the sect known as *pesharim*. In these works, the author follows along the Bible text — either from the Prophets or the Hagiographa —verse by verse, quoting the verses and then following by explaining each, beginning each explanation with the phrase *u'fishro* ("and its explanation ..."), hence the name given to these writings. It is the aim of the *pesharim* to show how the words of the verse have been fulfilled in the days of the author of the *pesher* (singular of *pesharim*). Thus we have a type of attempt to actualize the Biblical verses, where the verse in Psalms or in the Prophets is explained primarily as dealing with the history of the sect, its fate and its beliefs. According to the authors of the *pesharim*, the Biblical passages deal, among others, with the "Teacher of Righteousness," with the evil priests who are the enemies of the sect, with the terrible war that will take place in the eschatological future, and with similar topics. At the same time, we must admit that we cannot always understand the explanations given by the authors, as the language which they use is based on allusions and remains unclear to us.

This technique of bringing a verse and its explanation then the next verse and its explanation, reminds us — possibly only in terms of form — of things that we often find in the literature of our Sages. Most of the Midrashim which were created during the Tannaitic period, in the first 200 years of the Common Era (such as *Mekhilta* or *Sifra*) are based on a similar form: the Midrash deals with the Biblical book verse by verse; at first the verse or part of a verse is brought, and afterwards it is followed by an explanation, by expansion of the topic, by clarification, etc. The *Targums* (translations) of the Bible into Aramaic were also given in the same form: at first they would read the Biblical verse and afterwards they would translate and explain it, verse by verse. But the resemblance between the *Targum* and the Midrash on the one hand, and the *pesher* on the other, is only one of form, for there is a major difference between them in content.

Below is a *pesher* on Psalm 37:

"Those who wait for the Lord will possess the land" (37:9).

Its *pesher* — This is the congregation of His chosen ones who do His will.

"A little while and the wicked will be no more, you will look toward his place and he will not be there" (v. 10).

Its *pesher* — [This means that] all evil at the end of the forty years [will cease, and the wicked] will be no more.

"And the poor will inherit the land" (v. 11).

Its *pesher* — [This refers] to the poor who were saved from all the snares of Belial, and later will rejoice in all the good of the land.

It appears that the author of the *pesher* is explaining the three verses of the psalm as referring to his own sect (these being "the congregation of his chosen ones" and "the poor"), their enemies ("the wicked," "the snares of Belial"), and the future forty year war, which we have already mentioned above in reference to "the War between the Sons of Light and the Sons of Darkness".

We have in our possession fragments of *pesharim* on various psalms and on a number of books of the Prophets: Isaiah, Habakkuk, Micah and others. It would be logical to assume that the members of the sect were not the ones to devise this type of literary work, and that they merely adopted methods that were already common in the Jewish society before they left it.

In addition, there are other works which were found in the Dead Sea caves, which, although not having been authored by members of the sect, were preserved in their libraries. These works do not reflect the sect's views and beliefs, but rather the literary output of those days. Thus, for example, the scrolls include fragments, admittedly small, of a number of the apocryphal works, such as The Book of Jubilees or The Book of Enoch (with which we dealt in the second chapter), as well as fragments of the Aramaic *Targum* to a number of books of the Bible. Beyond these, a truly remarkable work was found there, possibly one of the pearls of Jewish creativity of all generations, a work which was labelled by those who published it, Yigael Yadin and Nahman Avigad, The Genesis Apocryphon. As we noted, this book does not reflect the special beliefs of the Dead Sea Sect, and it was only by purely fortuitous chance that it was preserved for posterity among the sect's treasures.

Unfortunately, the entire work did not reach us, and the vicissitudes of time caused considerable damage to the scroll. In terms of literary type it belongs to the broad group of Second Temple works that retell the Biblical story (also see above, Chapters 2 — 4). From what we are able to deduce, the scroll dealt with four individuals in the Book of Genesis: Lemech (and originally there

were those who wished to refer to this as "the Scroll of Lemech"),
Enoch, Noah and Abraham. It is written in the Aramaic of the 1st
century B.C.E..

A good part of whatever remained of the scroll deals with
Abraham. Abraham tells his readers — in the first person, as a
person writing an autobiography — his life story. We have already
encountered this type of writing in the apocryphal works: in The
Testaments of the Twelve Tribes (in which each of Jacob's sons
summarizes his life) or in The Book of Adam and Eve (where Eve
tells the story of the Garden of Eden from her point of view), and it
would appear that this type of story was relished by the people of
those generations.

In the section which, fortunately, was preserved almost in its
entirety, Abraham tells of his descent to Egypt and what happened
to him there. The basis for the text is the story in Genesis, Chapter
12 (verses 10—20). According to these verses, Abraham went
down to Egypt because of famine in Eretz Israel. As he feared the
Egyptians might kill him in order to take his beautiful wife, he asked
her to state that she was his sister. When they came to Egypt, Sarai
(as she was then known) was taken to the royal palace, whereas
Abraham received a great number of gifts from Pharaoh. God then
intervened and smote Pharaoh bodily, and he then realized that he
had been punished for taking Abraham's wife. Pharaoh returned
Sarai to her husband, and sent the two away from his country.

According to the scroll, though, that was not exactly what
occurred. When Abraham went down to Egypt — the author of the
scroll tells us — he had a dream. And these are his words:

I Abraham dreamed a dream on the night that we entered the
Land of Egypt. I saw in my dream that there stood a cedar tree
and a date palm tree, and people came who wished to cut down
and uproot the cedar and to leave the palm tree alone. The palm
cried out and said: "Do not cut down the cedar" ... and they left
the cedar alone because of the palm. I woke up at night from my
dream and I said to Sarai my wife: "I have dreamed a dream and
I am afraid because of that dream." She said to me: "Tell me
your dream and I will know." I then began telling her the dream.

66

As a result of the dream, Abraham and Sarah draw up a plan whereby they decide to conceal the fact that they are married, for the dream has shown them the danger awaiting Abraham and has even told them clearly that it will be through Sarah's words that Abraham will be saved from evil. A description such as this of the events evidently comes to explain a puzzling question about the Biblical account: Why did Abraham ask Sarah to pose as his sister? According to the Bible, he did so because of an unwarranted fear that he might be harmed; according to the scroll, he did so because he knew clearly about the danger which awaited him, and because he had been advised by God to conceal his relationship with Sarah. Thus the anonymous author modifies what appears to have been a lie told by Sarah and Abraham and presents it as proper behavior, which is justified based on the information available to the two.

One should note the comparison that the author brings, in quoting the dream, between Abraham and Sarah and the cedar and date palm. In a Midrash in our possession — which was composed hundreds of years after The Genesis Apocryphon — we find the story of Abraham and Sarah in Egypt (with a midrashic interpretation), which ends with the sentence, "About them [about Abraham and Sarah] it is said, 'The righteous shall flourish like the palm tree: he shall grow like a cedar in Lebanon'" (Ps. 92:13). One who reads this verse in the Midrash may find the juxtaposition of this verse with the story of Abraham and Sarah's descent to Pharaoh's Egypt surprising, but then along comes the scroll and shows us that there is an ancient tradition which links the verse in Psalms to the lives of Abraham and Sarah. This is further proof of the importance of the Second Temple era literature in obtaining a full understanding of the words of our Sages.

The author of the scroll then goes on to tell us how Abraham came to Egypt and how his wife was taken to the royal palace, after the king's ministers had seen her and had praised her to him. Here the author of the scroll brings us the detailed hymn of praise which Pharaoh's ministers sang to the king about Sarah. This is what they say to Pharaoh, describing Sarah from head to toe:

How beautiful are her eyes and how pleasant her nose and the radiance of her face ... How attractive her breasts and how pretty her whiteness [evidently a reference to her skin, which was lighter than that of the Egyptians]. How beautiful her hands and how perfect her arms ... How lovely her palms and how long and thin the fingers of her hands. Her legs how pretty and how perfect her thighs. None of the maidens and the brides who enter the bridal canopy is more beautiful than she, and her beauty exceeds that of all [other] women.

There is no need to note that nowhere will one find in the literature of our Sages as detailed a description of Sarah (or of any other woman), and one may surmise that it reflected the ideal of female beauty in the author's eyes.

Sarah was therefore taken forcibly to the royal palace. Unlike the Biblical account, though, which tells us of the many gifts that Pharaoh gave Abraham, the scroll entirely ignores this aspect. According to the scroll, Abraham gained nothing from the fact that his wife had been taken. He was not given sheep or cattle, camels or donkeys or servants. On the contrary, he stood and cried, cried out to the heavens and prayed (and there is no reference to this in the Bible). The description of the prayers of Abraham and of Lot, his nephew (who, incidentally, is not mentioned at all in the Torah in regard to Abraham's going down to Egypt) is among the most moving sections in the scroll.

God listens to Abraham's prayer and sends an evil wind which afflicts Pharaoh, his advisers and his physicians. For two years they suffer, and throughout that time Sarah remains in the royal palace. Throughout this entire time Pharaoh does not rape her or even approach her. The author of the scroll goes on to tell us what the Bible does not state specifically: nothing happened between Pharaoh and Abraham's wife, and she remained unviolated. After the two years of suffering, deliverance comes to Pharaoh from an unexpected quarter. One of his ministers, named Harkanosh, beseeches Lot to speak to Abraham and to ask him to aid the ailing king (the reason for this request is not given). Lot reveals to the minister the truth about Sarah, and Harkanosh hastens to tell the king what has caused the plague which has befallen him. The king is terrified, apologizes for his deeds and returns Sarah to Abraham with great honor. And here —and only here — does the author of the scroll tell us about the granting of gifts to Abraham. He does not receive them, as the Biblical account tells us, when his "sister" is taken from him, but only when Sarah is returned to him unharmed, as compensation for the suffering they have endured.

Among the numerous gifts which Abraham is given is Hagar, the Egyptian maidservant who later plays a significant part in the Biblical narrative. According to the author of the scroll, Hagar became part of Abraham's household when he went down to Egypt. It will also not be superfluous to mention that this tradition, too, appears in the literature of our Sages — but not necessarily in its most ancient works. Had we not had access to this scroll, we would not have been aware of the antiquity of this tradition.

We have thus seen how the author of the scroll retells the Biblical story, while changing it almost totally: Abraham and Sarah do not brazenly conceal the truth, but act in accordance with wise advice given them from heaven; Abraham is not rewarded for the fact that Sarah is taken, and his wife's chastity is scrupulously maintained. It appears that the author of the scroll and his readers found no difficulty in accepting what it contains, and did not regard it as being in contradiction to the Biblical account.

VI.

The Ancient Mystical Works

When we speak of the mystical works, we refer to various literary creations or realms of thought which have occupied an important and distinct place in human existence in general and in the Judaic milieu in particular. It would appear that throughout Jewish cultural history there has existed — either openly or in secret — a world of various mystical views. Such a world already existed before the period of our Sages, at the end of the Biblical period, in the Second Temple period and afterwards. The relationship between the world of mysticism and the other spheres of Jewish culture changed from era to era and took on different and changing forms.

The world of mysticism, being foreign to our routine daily existence, is an enchanted and attractive world, but also a very complex one, with many faces and forms, and the different domains within it cannot be easily partitioned into separate entities. One must therefore be very careful in any attempt at generalization, such as the one we will be presenting below. At the same time, though, it appears that one can divide the different mystical views in Judaism that co-existed side-by-side with the world of our Sages into three basic groups: the apocalyptic literature, the *hekhalot* ("palaces") literature, and the magic literature.

The *apocalyptic* literature is religious literature (and one can bring examples of it from other religions as well), which primarily contains prophecies or visions of what will come to pass at the End of Days, and, to a lesser extent, other secrets which are generally concealed from human view, such as what happens in other worlds, Paradise and Gehenna, Satan, angels and spirits, etc. This type of literature is especially popular at times of national crises, when the need is felt to flee from the burdensome and bitter present to sweet and intoxicating descriptions of a more promising and better future or of beautiful and radiant worlds which parallel ours. This literature includes parts of the Biblical Daniel — who lived in the Hellenistic era — as well as a considerable portion of the apocryphal books. An example of the latter is *The Book of Enoch*, which deals primarily with Enoch's voyages to higher worlds, revealing their secrets and what occurs there (see Chapter 2 above).

Another apocryphal work, most of which deals with apocalyptic ideas, is the work known as *IV Esdras*. This book, which was evidently written close to the destruction of the Second Temple, gives detailed descriptions of the catastrophes which will yet occur, cosmic calamities that will rock the world and will prepare the basis for a new era, a better one that will begin with the destruction of the world as it is now. Thus, for example, the author of the work describes the future:

> Days will come and the sun will suddenly shine in the night and the moon during the day. The trees will drip blood and the rocks will cry out ... The Sodom (i.e., Dead) Sea will produce fish ... and will shout at night. Fire will burst out time after time and the animals of the field will move from their places. Women will give birth to monsters and sweet water will give forth bitter (Chapter 5).

This is a description of a total reversal of the laws of nature, where the natural laws will be replaced by their opposites.

When the author of *IV Esdras* wishes to depict the Day of Judgment, he uses vivid, semi-poetic language, proclaiming:

For the Day of Judgment is thus —
There will be no sun nor moon nor stars
No cloud and no lightning and no thunder
No wind and no water and no air
No darkness and no evening and no morning
No summer and no seedtime and no winter

No harvest and no heat and no cold
No hail and no dew and no rain
No moon and no night and no dawn
No light and no brightness and no radiance
But only the splendor of the glory of the Supreme (*Ibid.* 7)

Following this description, the author goes on to describe the radiant Jerusalem on High which will descend to the earth and will thereby open a new, better era.

Among the scrolls of the Dead Sea sect, too, one finds elements that belong to the apocalyptic literature. One should especially mention The War between the Sons of Light with the Sons of Darkness, a work which gives a description of a war in the apocalyptic future between the forces of darkness and their opponents, "the Sons of Light." (This work was discussed in the previous chapter.)

One can also find apocalyptic elements in the literature of our Sages — descriptions of the Garden of Eden and the war between Leviathan and the Wild Ox in the presence of the righteous, a description of Gehenna and the punishments to be endured by the wicked, the events expected to occur in the apocalyptic future, such as the Day of Judgment, the coming of the Messiah, the revival of the dead, the descent of Jerusalem on High to the earth, etc. But these descriptions in the literature of our Sages do not generally give any indication of the imminent approach of these events, whereas the apocalyptic literature is steeped in the belief that the events being described are to take place very soon, before the eyes of the writer and readers. As mentioned, the apocalyptic literature flourishes at times of national crisis (such as the destruction of the Temple or the ascent of Islam), and hence its imminent character, which loses a great deal of its potency when the political and social conditions change. In most cases, when our Sages deal with apocalyptic topics, this imminent dimension is missing.

The second group of mystical works at the time of our Sages is the *Hekhalot* literature, which describes spiritual voyages toward a mystical union with God, whereas the third group is the *magic* literature, which teaches the individual how to exploit the secret information to which he has access in order to influence events in this world. We will deal with both of these groups at greater length later on, after we state a few general principles about all three groups as a whole. (Incidentally, we have decided not to include one category of works, which some of the readers may feel is relevant to the topic at hand, and here I refer to the kabbalistic literature in general and to the *Zohar* in general. It is true that the traditional view is that the *Zohar* was written by Tanna'im in the 2nd century C.E., namely R' Simeon bar Johai and his colleagues, and if that is so this work belongs here, but scientific research does not accept this view, and regards the *Zohar* as being a medieval creation. It indeed utilizes ancient traditions, some of which extend back to the period of our Sages, but it is primarily after the time of our Sages and we will therefore not deal with it.)

What do the three categories we have mentioned have in common? I would venture to say in this regard that there are two features which unite them. First, there is their esoteric nature. They are not meant for the masses, and only a few special individuals in each generation may know and deal with these topics. Before doing so, the mystic must undergo exhaustive preparatory training and must be blessed with those qualities which enable him to deal with these lofty secrets, some of which may even be dangerous. In addition, in order to preserve their esoteric nature, the mystical texts are generally written in language which cannot be understood easily by those not familiar with it. Sometimes the texts are ambiguous: the mystic reads and understands them one way (which he believes is the correct way), whereas a person unfamiliar with mysticism will understand them entirely differently.

The second common attribute of all the mystical works which we have mentioned is that they deal with other worlds, either in terms of time (i.e., events that will take place at some future time, such as the End of Days and the coming of the messiah, etc.), or in terms of place (worlds which parallel our own — the Garden of Eden or the world of the angels, etc.). In either case, the texts do not deal directly with the world in which the mystic finds himself here and now. Thus these texts give the person the opportunity to flee from reality, freeing him from the present and allowing him to deal with far-away matters, secrets of the future or other worlds. As a result, the present-day reality in which the mystic finds himself assumes a different character. It is true that the mystics' legs walk on this world, but their eyes and their thoughts are in other worlds — the important ones — and it is in light of these worlds that the mystics explain what is happening to them and to all of humanity.

It is in these two aspects that the literature of our Sages differs totally from that of the mystics. It is not hidden or meant for isolated individuals. On the contrary, it is available to whoever wishes to study it and to assume full mastery of it. The *derashot* in the synagogue about the Torah or the Torah translation into Aramaic were geared to all the people, the young were educated in school, eulogies were delivered at funerals, speeches offered best wishes at weddings. In all of these circumstances the sages imparted freely of their knowledge to the masses. There was never an attempt (except in truly unusual circumstances) to disguise the words with difficult or unclear language. Whoever is thirsty — let him come to the water and drink! The study hall is never locked for those who wish to study the Torah.

And if we stated that the different types of mystical works deal primarily with other worlds and enable their readers to find refuge from the turmoil of the world, the literature of our Sages differs tremendously from them in this as well. Our Sages dealt first and foremost with the world in which they and their audience lived: how were they to act in various *halakhic* questions? What are the proper character traits of a person? How should one react to these or other problems? The Sages' involvement in other worlds generally came to further their major aims. The descriptions of the reward for the righteous in the Garden of Eden, for example, could help strengthen the hands of those who were lax in their observance of the commandments, whereas a description of the bitter fate of the other nations on the Day of Judgment gave the Jew who was oppressed by a foreign government the power to survive in a foreign and hostile world. We do not find in the literature of our Sages a

74

retreat from reality, or, for that matter, an attempt to nullify or despise it.

One of the differences between the world of the mystics and that of the literature of our Sages is expressed, for example, in examining their angelology — i.e., by examining the angels portrayed in them. In all three types of mystical literature with which we are dealing, one will find a plethora of angels, each having its own unique and often bizarre name (for examples of these, see below), which construct a clearly hierarchical society, and which have clearly defined duties. It is true that the literature of our Sages also describes angels — and some even have names: Michael, Gabriel, Raphael, etc. — but the angelology of our Sages pales into insignificance when compared to that of the mystics. One who examines *Malakhei Elyon* ("The Heavenly Angels") by Reuven Margolioth — a type of lexicon of angels as they appear in the Jewish literature throughout the generations — will see immediately that the literature of our Sages is put in the shadow when compared to the mystical literature and its references to angels.

At the same time, one should not hurry to describe the literature of our Sages as being in total opposition to the mystical literature. There is no doubt that some of our sages were also involved in mysticism, and it is only natural that signs of this remained in their literature. This is especially apparent when our Sages deal with the creation of the world or with the descriptions of God's appearing to the Jewish people and its prophets. When dealing with these two categories and similar ones, we find intertwined within the words of the Sages statements which are derived from the mystical realm, but the number of these in the totality of our Sages' creativity — the two Talmuds and the different Midrashim — is not great. In this context, it is worthwhile noting that the scientific study of the literature of our Sages and of ancient Jewish mysticism recognizes opposite positions on this question: there are those who magnify the importance and the role played by mysticism in the literature of our Sages and those who limit it greatly. At the same time, it appears to me that both will agree that, as a rule, we do not find mysticism playing a decisive role in the literature of our Sages.

Now we will return to two of the categories of mysticism that we mentioned above, the *hekhalot* literature and the magic literature, and we will expand on the topic.

The *hekhalot* literature is a Jewish literature (and it would appear that there is nothing exactly like it in other religions) whose origin is in the group of mystics that were known as *yordei merkavah* ("those who ascend the Chariot"). This group existed approximately from the 2nd to the 7th centuries C.E. This literature deals primarily with a very detailed description of a spiritual and mystical voyage to the higher worlds. The Chariot is God's Chariot, in which He appeared to the prophet Ezekiel, as described in the prophecies at the beginning of that book. One who "ascends the Chariot" cuts himself off from his present-day existence and departs for a long journey into the recesses of the heavens or *hekhalot* ("palaces"), a trip which will eventually bring him to a complete mystical unification with God. A considerable portion of this literature is devoted to instructions to those who wish to embark on this complex voyage: what they must take with them and when they must depart, what dangers lie along the road and how to react if one comes into contact with these, what the password is at each point and what sights can be seen along the way, and so on. In the end, one will reach the last *hekhal*, the seventh, and there the journey will end. This is a linguistic and literary expression of a mystical experience that any person who is not a mystic cannot fully understand. He can read the texts, more or less understand the description or events or the different words, can follow the sequence of events, but cannot undergo the spiritual experience behind the written text. Only one who knows how to elevate himself above and beyond the word, and to achieve the mystical state which the words are meant to represent, can understand fully this voyage to the uppermost reaches.

The heroes of the *hekhalot* literature, those people who set out on the arduous and dangerous voyage, are individuals known to us from the literature of our Sages, such as R' Akiva and his contemporary, R' Ishmael. But it would appear that in the final analysis this is no more than a literary device using familiar and well-known names. Very well known is the Talmudic tradition (over whose correct interpretation a long and strenuous argument has raged) about "the four that entered *pardes*" ("orchard" — *Hagigah* 14b):

> Ben Azzai looked and died ... Ben Zoma looked and was injured (i.e., he evidently lost his mind) ... Aher (literally "the other" — Elisha ben Avuyah, the teacher of R' Meir — referred to thus in order to avoid mention of him by name) mutilated the plants (i.e., became a heretic) ... R' Akiva entered in peace and emerged in peace.

The *hekhalot* literature is built on the idea of that entry and exit, as it describes the path a person should follow if he wishes to reach his destination in peace and also to emerge from it without being harmed. It appears that the circle of those who went out in the Chariot was very close to the circles from which the literature of our Sages emerged — and it is possible that some of these mystics were of our Sages — thus the closeness of the two groups.

Below is a passage from *Sefer Hekhalot Rabbati*, one of the works which we have today from those circles. The speaker is R' Ishmael, who guides his readers:

> When you come and stand at the entrance of the first *hekhal*, take two seals in your two hands, one of Tutrosiaiyoi and one of Suria, the minister of the interior. Show that of Tutrosiaiyoi to those standing on the right and that of Suria to those standing on the left. Immediately Kahabiel, the minister who is in charge of the entrance to the first *hekhal*, stands to the right of the doorpost, and Topahiel the minister stands to the left of the doorpost ... and they will take you and hand you over and notify Tagriel, the minister who is in charge of the entrance to the second *hekhal*, etc.

At that point, the person has to show other seals or recite various formulations, by which he will be able to continue on his journey. As we mentioned above, we can read the words and try to describe the voyage in earthly terms, but the spiritual and mystical experience behind these descriptions remains beyond our understanding.

Below follows a description of the meeting with God in the last *hekhal*:

> As the man wishes to ascend the Chariot, Anaphael opens up the entrance to the seventh *hekhal*, and it is filled with eyes, each of the holy eyes the size of a large sieve, and the eyes appear as lightning flashes ... The man is shaken and fearful and confused and frightened, and falls backward.

Here we have a description of a mystical ecstasy which one can understand word for word, yet without experiencing its tremendous force.

This entire literary group is generally regarded as including one other work, which the modern reader will find very difficult to read. That is the volume entitle *Shi'ur Komah*, a short work dedicated to a description of God and indicating His size. God is described here in entirely human physical terms, and the volume gives a detailed description of His face, His nose, His nostrils, etc., with each individual part and its measurement, together with various Hebrew letter combinations which we do not understand. Here too, the same warning is appropriate: the reader of this work is liable to regard it as being bizarre or even ludicrous, but one should remember that the feelings experienced by the mystical reader escape us. Gershom Scholem, the greatest scholar of the ancient kabbalah, believes that *Shi'ur Komah* was written in the 1st or 2nd centuries C.E. in Eretz Israel, i.e., at the same time and in the same place where the Mishnah was created. It would thus appear that this works, too, was written around the study halls of our Sages!

We will conclude by mentioning the *magic* literature, whose primary goal was instruction in the proper usage of supernatural information in man's hands in order to help him in this world. One who knows the supernatural truth can utilize it in order to influence this world: to heal the sick and cause the barren to give birth, to banish evil spirits and to ensure success in horse racing, to implant love in a woman's heart or to kill an enemy, etc. In order to be successful in all of these, the person has to carry out certain magic acts, using various objects (such as a dead mouse that was preserved in old wine for three years) at specific times (such as on the 15th of the month, when the moon is at its brightest), while uttering various prayers and oaths.

An important work, as far as we are concerned, is *Sefer ha-Razim*. This was written in elegant Hebrew, and it is customarily regarded as an Eretz Israel work of the 3rd century C.E. Its source is undoubtedly among Jewish circles, and it is interesting to see how there were among them men who believed in the power of calling upon angels, of the pouring of wine or the slaughtering of a white rooster in the angels' honor, etc. Mordecai Margalioth, who published the book (Jerusalem 1966), admits that he did so with a heavy heart, for as a religious Jew he found it hard to believe that such circles existed at more or less the same time and in the same place as our Sages.

Here is one example from *Sefer ha-Razim*, meant for a person who wishes a certain woman to love a specific man:

If you wish to place the love of a man in a woman's heart, take two copper trays, and write the names of the following angels on both their sides: Azaziel, Hananel, Pazaziel, Yeshaiel, Dalkiel, Arpada ... and the name of the man and the name of the woman, and say the following: I ask of you the angels who rule over the constellations of the children of Adam and Eve, that you do my will and draw the man's constellation close to the woman, that he find favor in her eyes. (2:29—30)

Man's knowledge of the angelic system in the Upper Worlds and his knowledge of the names of the angels who are in charge of this task, thus aids him to realize his wishes in this world.

And one who wishes to know in which month he will die is to do the following:

Take platters of refined gold and make twelve tablets of each, and write on each the name of an angel and his month. Then take good oil seven years old and throw all the tablets in it. Then recite the following oath seven times over the oil and say: "I make you, the angels of knowledge and erudition swear ... I make you swear to inform me of the month of my death ..."

79

Then place the oil under the stars for seven nights in a new glass vessel ... And on the seventh night get up at midnight and look in the oil, and see which tablet floats on the oil and what month is written on it. In that month you will die.

In the literature of our Sages, we also find allusions to magical practices in which the Jewish people engaged. So too is there archaeological evidence, such as amulets (which we will mention in the following chapters), which informs us of the place occupied by magic in the culture of the time, primarily in the folk culture. It is with the background of all these that we are also to understand the literature of our Sages. An ostrich policy, which deals with our ancient literature while ignoring the various mystical views which were prevalent at the time and their literary expression, cannot serve one in searching for the truth.

VII.

Archaeology and Art

Up to now we have dealt with literary texts which reached us in writing, and which either preceded or were coterminous with the literature of our Sages. But it would appear that if one wishes to understand fully the world which surrounded our Sages, he should utilize the data supplied by archaeology and ancient art.

In this chapter, I intend to deal with non-verbal evidence for aggadic traditions, in the preservation of aggadic traditions in mosaics, pictures, statues, inscriptions, etc. It appears that various archaeological discoveries and artistic works which adorn museums throughout the world reflect in their own ways narrative motifs, beliefs and opinions (as well as a broad range of philological, historical and cultural information, which we will also mention in brief), whose roots go back to the era of our Sages, and which one cannot ignore in our discussion.

Let us begin with *pictures*. In about 1930, there were discovered among the ruins of the city Dura-Europos along the Euphrates (the present-day Iraqi-Syrian border) the remnants of a synagogue that had been destroyed — together with the rest of the city — in about 255 C.E. The archaeologists who worked on the site were delighted to find that along the entire length of its walls there were colored drawings that had been painted on plaster. But these were not pictures of flowers or abstract designs. Instead, they found various Biblical scenes: Jacob's dream, Moses being drawn from the water, the splitting of the Sea of Reeds, David being anointed by Samuel,

Solomon's Temple, the miracle of *Purim*, and various other scenes. Some of the drawings even had Aramaic captions explaining them: "Moses splitting the Sea of Reeds," "Samuel anointing David," etc. It appears that the builders and decorators of the synagogue were not over-scrupulous about the prohibition in the Ten Commandments, "You shall not make a graven image or any likeness" (or interpreted it leniently), and saw nothing wrong with decorating the synagogue with drawings of Biblical figures and their deeds. So too was it found that the drawings not only describe the Biblical tradition, but go beyond it by using narrative motifs known to us from the written aggadic literature. Thus we have clear evidence of the existence of these aggadic traditions in the middle of the 3rd century C.E., and at a considerable distance from Eretz Israel, the birthplace of the aggadah. And we should remember that the illustrator of those days did not paint (on either cloth or a wall) his own personal impressions but wished to have his drawings understood by all, and as such he had to be sure to draw topics which all would recognize. The date of the destruction of the synagogue is thus the latest date for the tradition as described in these drawings, and we may assume that even before the artist began to work, the tradition which he planned to depict was already a matter of common knowledge.

We will now bring an aggadah which appears in a 13th century work, *Yalkut Shimoni*, and in other late works. Its expanded version which we will quote was revealed among Midrashic fragments published by Saul Lieberman. This aggadah deals with a marginal Biblical figure, Hiel the Bethelite, who is mentioned in I Kings (16:34) for having disregarded Joshua's prohibition and having rebuilt Jericho. According to the aggadah, Hiel denied both the Torah and God, and gave himself over to the idolatry practiced by Isabel on Mount Carmel. "When Elijah came to Ahab to test the prophets of Baal and the priests of the high places" — the famous story of the contest between Elijah and the prophets of Baal in bringing down fire from heaven (I Kings 18), the Midrash tells us:

> The prophets of Baal knew that Baal did not have the ability to produce fire of himself. What did Hiel do? He stood opposite the prophets of Baal and said to them: "Strengthen yourselves

and stand opposite Elijah and I will do something which will make it appear as if Baal is sending you fire." What did he do? He took two stones in his hand and flax tinder and went inside the statue of Baal, which was hollow, and he smote the stones one against the other in order to light the tinder. Elijah immediately realized (what was happening), by Divine inspiration, and he said to Him (i.e., to God): "Lord of the Universe ... I ask that you kill that evil man in the bowels of Baal." The Holy One, blessed be He, immediately commanded a snake, which bit him on the heel and he died.

Whoever reads this aggadah in *Yalkut Shimoni* or in other works of the geonic period sees no reason to assume that it was composed many centuries earlier. The language of the aggadah, too, indicates that it is a late work, and prevents anyone from dating this tradition in the ancient past. Yet the archaeologists were amazed to find that, among the many drawings on the walls of the synagogue in Dura-Europos, there is a picture of people wearing long clothes standing around a square hollow structure (the altar), in which a small man holds something round, with a large snake approaching him from his right side. There is no doubt that the artist is referring to the Biblical story of Elijah and the prophets of Baal, together with the tradition of Hiel hiding in the bowels of the statue of Baal and being bitten by a snake. And if this is what the artist wished to portray in the middle of the 3rd century C.E., it must mean that the tradition which he preserved was of even earlier origin, for a period of time had to pass until the aggadic tradition became a commonly known one.

This picture thus is conclusive evidence of the antiquity of the above tradition, at least of the latter days of the Tannaitic period, even though its first appearance in writing is hundreds of years later. When one deals with oral literature, only part of which is ever committed to writing (and even this in a comparatively random fashion), one is liable to find numerous examples of ancient traditions that were handed down orally for many generations, and only transcribed much later. The picture with which we have dealt here is an instructive example of this process; in the absence of the drawings on the Dura-Europos synagogue, we might have regarded the tradition about Hiel in the late Midrashim as a medieval creation, and we would have made a grievous error.

In the drawing of Moses being drawn from the river, one can see Pharaoh's daughter's maidservants standing by her at the river, while a naked woman stands in the water, holding an infant in her left hand and a small ark in the water to her right. This, of course, is a representation of what the Torah writes (Ex. 2:5), "And the daughter of Pharaoh came down to wash herself at the river ... and she sent her maid (*amata* in Hebrew) to fetch it" (i.e., the ark). Yet in the Midrash there are various views of the meaning of the word *amata*. As there is no vocalization in the Torah text, the word can equally be understood to mean "her hand." Onkelos (whom we will yet deal with), in his Aramaic translation of the Torah, understands it as a maid, whereas another Aramaic translation, attributed to Jonathan ben Uziel, explains it as if it indeed refers to the hand. The person who painted the synagogue in Dura-Europos obviously could not depict both views, and had to choose between them. He thus chose the one which understands it to mean her maidservant, and therefore gave clear expression to the interpretation which he knew. If one then wishes to list the different holders of views of the meaning of the word *amata*, one must include the anonymous painter of Dura-Europos with Onkelos (and the others who follow this view) as all maintaining the same interpretation.

From all the above, it follows that traditions which are reflected in pictures without having been expressed in the literature of our Sages may not have been the product of the imagination of the painter, but evidence of the existence of an aggadic tradition which was forgotten over the course of time. That, for example, is the case with the miracle of the waters of Marah (Ex. 15). In this picture, we see Moses, bearded, throwing a rod into a round body of water like a well, and from the body of water flow twelve streams of water to twelve tents, which clearly represent the Twelve Tribes of Israel. No where in the literature of our Sages do we find a written aggadic tradition which mentions the waters of Marah splitting into twelve springs, with each tribe having its own spring. It is true that there is a similar tradition about the well of Miriam, and one can claim that the painter transferred it to this story, but it would appear to me more logical to claim that the painter was aware of such a tradition in regard to the waters of Marah as well, and gave expression to this in his painting. This particular tradition was never written down in the literature of our Sages, and we have already had occasion to mention the random character of the transcription of the words of the Midrash. If we may be permitted to use our imaginative capability somewhat, we can hypothesize the existence of a midrash along the following lines (Ex. 15:25), "'The Lord showed him a tree, which when he had cast into the waters, and the waters were made sweet' — our Sages said: The waters became separate streams. There are those who say: twelve, as the number of the tribes of Israel, and others say ...'' etc. As I understand it, even if we have not (yet) found such a midrash in writing, one cannot question its existence, following the finding of this wall painting.

Archeology yields a great deal of additional information, in the archeology of synagogues and especially in the *inscriptions* that are found in them. A large number of inscriptions have been found in the ruins of tens of synagogues, both in Eretz Israel and outside it, from which we are able to glean important linguistic and historical information. The linguistic aspect is of inestimable value, for the inscriptions are living evidence of the vocabulary, spelling and syntax in effect at the time that these synagogues were built. Most of the texts of the language of our Sages that we possess are dated to a period after the time they were written (they reached us after a long series of repeated copying and editing), and one who wishes to see actual texts as they were written in those days will find in these inscriptions a veritable treasure. The historic information that they supply is also of great importance: the inscriptions reveal to us the places where Jews lived, list their names, tell us what languages they spoke (the inscriptions are in Hebrew, Aramaic or Greek), what they did for a living, etc. In the town of Dabura in the Golan, for example, a stone was found upon which was written: "This is the study hall of Rabbi Eliezer ha-Kappar." That is remarkable evidence of the existence of that scholar and of where he lived, or at the least that a study hall had been named after him.

Most of the inscriptions in the synagogues are dedications, in which the artist or the donor who funded or built the synagogue or parts of it or special items used in the service is mentioned, such as a dedication in the mosaic floor of Kfar Kana (which appears in Aramaic): "May he be remembered for good, Jose ben Tanhum ben Botah and his sons who made this tablet. May this be for them a blessing. Amen." This short inscription about those who built the tablet or who paid for the work, teaches us about names in use at the time, or a possible meaning of the word *tavlah* (which we translated above as "tablet," in this case referring to the mosaic floor) and on the use of the expression, "May it be for them a blessing. Amen."

But some of the inscriptions do not only supply information of this type, which — as mentioned — is of great value in itself, but deal with *halakhic* or other issues, such as the curse *qua* oath in the mosaic in the synagogue in Ein Gedi (and here the text is in Aramaic):

Whoever causes arguments between a person and his fellow
Or who slanders his fellow to the non-Jews
Or who steals his fellow's property
Or who reveals the secrets of the city to non-Jews —
The One whose eyes wander over all the earth ...
Will turn His face to that person and his descendants
And will uproot him from beneath the heavens
And may all the people say amen and amen, selah.

Scholars differ as to the meaning of "the secrets of the city" mentioned here, about which this oath was written. It appears that the most likely meaning is that those who "reveal the secrets of the city" is a reference to the secret of the manufacture of balsam perfume, which was the pride of the population of Ein Gedi, and which they wished to prevent others from knowing. Regardless of whether this is the meaning or not, this inscription enables us to peer directly into the world of our fathers, their relationships with non-Jews, and the special relationship which they maintained among themselves. The inscription also shows an interesting use of language, for "the One whose eyes wander over all the earth" is an expression which is based on Zechariah 4:10, and this shows that the verses of the Bible were in constant use by the people of those generations. Furthermore, we learn of the use of the formulation, "amen and amen, selah," which evidently was meant to signify assent to an oath.

In addition, at the top of the above inscription in Ein Gedi we find, among others, the names "Abraham, Isaac, and Jacob," as well as "Hananiah, Mishael and Azariah." Scholars have also debated why these names are here. It appears, though, that one of the Midrashim contains a sentence which was very difficult to understand until this inscription was found, and this is a beautiful example of how archeology and the study of the Midrash help one another. We refer here to *Shir Ha-Shirim Rabbah*, which states: "People are accustomed to swearing by He who established the world on the three pillars. There are those who say: Abraham, Isaac and Jacob. Others say: Hananiah, Mishael and Azariah." Thus we see that there were people, such as those of Ein Gedi, who would seek to strengthen their oaths by mentioning the three forefathers or the three friends of Daniel (who were thrown into the burning furnace with him) as witnesses. Now we find this practice corroborated by two sources, both in the Midrash and in the inscription in Ein Gedi.

The archeological digs of synagogues also supplied the answer to another question. Only once in the literature of our Sages do we find the expression "the *katedra* (i.e., chair) of Moses," and we are even told that it had "a round head" (*Pesikta d'Rav Kahana* 1:10). This expression is found one other time in Matthew (23:2). It was customary to assume that both were references to a special chair in the synagogue, upon which the elder of the congregation, the *parnas* (lay head), or its greatest scholar sat, and that the chair was named such because the person who sat in it was considered to be the one who continued in the ways of the giver of the Torah and its first interpreter. Indeed, archeological digs have shown the existence of a chair which fits the description in the Midrash, such as the one found in the synagogue in Tiberias: a chair with a rounded top, carved out of white chalk rock, where the person sat facing the people (even though his back was to the holy ark), evidence of his special status. Here too archeology and the Midrashic text illuminate one another.

In other synagogues and buildings, the archaeologists also found *mosaics*. These mosaics sometimes depict the zodiacal signs (and even list them by name). Sometimes they have actual pictures, such as the famous mosaic in the synagogue of Bet Alfa, which depicts the story of the sacrifice of Isaac. One can clearly see in it Abraham and the large knife in his hand, Isaac, and the youths sitting next to the ass, the hand of God (or the angel) coming from heaven and the ram tied to the bush. Alongside most of the figures there is an inscription which explains who the person is. Thus we can see that not only in far-off Dura-Europos did they have no hesitation in decorating a synagogue with drawings of people.

The Bet Alfa mosaic is also interesting from another point of view. In the literature of our Sages there is a dispute regarding Isaac's age at the time of his sacrifice; there are those who claim he was a small, innocent child, who was brought as a sheep to the slaughter and had no idea what fate his father had in store for him. The others, though — and that is the more commonly accepted view — hold that he was 37 years old. This figure is deduced by the desire to portray Isaac as an adult who went to what he thought was his death with the full knowledge of that fact, and not as a child led blindly by a pitiless father. Such a description of the events can serve the aim (which developed as a result of various historical processes) to regard Isaac as the archetype of those who sanctify God's name by their actions, people who go to their deaths with their eyes wide open and out of love for God and the readiness to carry out the will of their Creator.

The establishment of Isaac's age as 37 is aided by the Biblical account: the story of Sarah's death at the age of 127 appears in the Torah (Gen. 23) immediately after the story of the sacrifice of Isaac (Gen. 22), which made it possible to claim that it was the sacrifice which brought about Isaac's mother's broken heart and her subsequent death. However, as Sarah had been 90 years old when

Isaac was born, one must state that Isaac was 37 when his mother died. Yet the mosaic in Bet Alfa depicts Isaac as a small child — and this is proof that at the time of the artisan (the 5th or 6th century C.E.) and in his place, a minority opinion was also current which regarded Isaac as a small child.

In this regard, we should mention another mosaic, which has a drawing of another Biblical figure. I refer here to the mosaic in the synagogue of Gaza, in which David appears (next to the figure wearing a crown there appears the word "David") playing a string instrument, where various animals skip about him and listen to his playing. The many traditions about King David as "the sweet singer of Israel," as the one who wrote the Book of Psalms, and as the one who had a stringed instrument suspended above his bed, are to be seen here in a special way and in a forceful manner, for which I have found no parallel in the sources. This description was presumably drawn from Greek art, which pictured Orpheus along similar lines. It is interesting to note that in this mosaic we find the stringed instrument which David is holding containing fifteen strings. In the midrashic literature (such as *Tanhuma* [Buber], *Beha'alot'kha* 12) there is a dispute about the number of strings: there are those who say there were seven and other who say there were eight. I do not know if in this case the anonymous artist chose the number fifteen (which is the sum of seven and eight) deliberately, or if this was a coincidence. Either way, to answer the question of how many strings there were in David's string instrument, one can either resort to the Midrash or to the mosaic here.

We should also mention briefly the many types of *amulets*, which teach us about the world of beliefs (general folk beliefs) of the time — magical incantations, etc. (and see the previous chapter). Some of these amulets contain the famous *Magen David* six-pointed star, the expression "abracadabra" (our predecessors believed that this brought relief to toothache and fever), and Moses' name, for example, to which they attributed extensive magical powers. We would not have known anything about these or about others like them from the literature of our Sages alone.

The World of the Aggadah

We will conclude this review with drawings and sculptures of a later time, which, because of their need to interpret, to provide details and to represent concretely, either reflect aggadic traditions or are the basis for new traditions. Thus, for example, there is the universally known tradition that what Eve gave Adam was an apple. This tradition has absolutely no basis in the Bible, where it simply states "the fruit of the tree." One who searches the sources will find that the literature of our Sages contains a number of different views of what the fruit was: there are those who say that it was the citron (a fruit known for its sexual symbolism), while others say it was a fig (and it was fig leaves that Adam and Eve sewed together to cover their nakedness — only the tree that caused them to sin would help them overcome the results of the sin). Others hold it was a grape vine (telling us, as it were, that the grape, source of wine and drunkenness, was what brought sin to the world), or even wheat. The apple came from the Christian artistic tradition, which found its way into illuminated Hebrew manuscripts in the Middle Ages, such as prayer books and *haggadot*. The same is true for many statues and paintings (such as Michelangelo's famous statue) that depict Moses as having small horns growing from his forehead. It would appear that we have here a transformation of meanings, whereby the statement about Moses in Ex. 34:30, "the skin of his face shone (*karan* in Hebrew)," is taken not to refer to rays of light, but literally to a horn (*keren* in Hebrew) or horns. The source of this may be the Vulgate translation of the Bible, for that is how it translated the passage, or it may be that this was not an innovation of the translator but rather relied on a Jewish tradition, which is documented in various ancient Aramaic poems, in which Moses tells the angels that he will gore them with his horns if they prevent him from ascending Mount Sinai. Finally, the prophet Jonah is represented in medieval European sculptures as a bald, completely hairless man. One may be able to say that this is a transformation of a tradition in the Midrash, that it was tremendously hot inside the belly of the fish that swallowed Jonah. The ancients may have assumed that heat such as this had to cause physical damage such as the loss of one's hair, and that is why they depicted Jonah as being bald.

One can therefore conclude from the above that paintings and sculptures, inscriptions and mosaics enrich our knowledge of the aggadic world of our Sages, are evidence of the widespread knowledge of the aggadic tradition in the cultural world of the time, or aid us in ascertaining the date it was created. These are thus direct, non-mediated aids in having a live contact with times past.

VIII.

Folk Literature

In *Midrash Tanhuma*, (on Genesis, Section 11), which is one of the Midrashim on the Torah, the following story is brought:

Lamech was his (Cain's) descendant, and was of the seventh generation, and was blind. He would go out to hunt with his son holding him by the hand. When the child saw him, he said: "I see a type of animal." He drew his bow in that direction and killed Cain. The child saw him from afar dead, with a horn in his forehead. He said to Lamech: "My father, I see a figure of a man that has been killed, with a horn in his forehead." Lamech said: "Woe to me! He is my ancestor!" He clapped his two hands together in remorse and hit the child's head, killing him accidentally, as it states (Gen. 4:23), "I have slain a man to my wounding, and a young man to my hurt." That evening, [Lamech's] wives went out after him and found their ancestor (i.e., Cain) dead and their son Tubal-Cain dead.

This aggadah is brought by the scholar Louis Ginzberg as an instructive example of the interesting merger that is sometimes created in the literature of our Sages between the Midrashic activity which was the product of the sages in the study halls, and the folk creations, whose source was among broad groups of the Jewish people. One who reads this aggadah will see that, among others, it deals with the content of Biblical verses and attempts to explain them. Lamech's short and puzzling poem (Gen. 4:23), "I have slain a man to my wounding, and a young man to my hurt," is explained as referring to two murders: that of Cain ("a man" in the verse, and indeed, when Cain was born, Eve exclaimed [Gen. 4:1], "I have gotten a man from the Lord"), and that of "a young man," Tubal Cain. The sages who read this verse asked who the "man" and the "young man" were, and determined that they were individuals of the literary and historical environment of Lamech: his ancestor seven generations removed, and his son. As the Torah states in regard to Cain (Gen. 4:15), "Vengeance shall be taken on him sevenfold," a difficult expression referring to the vengeance that will come upon Cain for having slain Abel, they, as it were, "killed two birds with one stone," and referred the above verse to the seventh generation, namely Lamech. At the same time, this aggadah expresses a number of folk motifs known to us from international folklore in general, such as that of the blind hunter who shoots with the aid of another person who directs him, a description of the powerful man who is able to kill a child accidentally merely by clapping his hands, or a description of the horn on Cain's forehead, which led Tubal Cain to mistake him for an animal.

This horn is clearly a folk explanation of the "sign" that God gave to Cain, after He punished him with being forced to wander and be in exile (Gen. 4:15). In the Midrashim we find a number of interpretations of the nature of that sign, such as leprosy which broke out on Cain's forehead, or a dog which Cain was given to guard him. According to another interpretation, God made the sun set early (it was Friday) so that the Sabbath would begin earlier than normal. That was a sign to Cain that God had forgiven him. And there are various other explanations. The horn which grew out of Cain's forehead was evidently the folk rendition of the nature of that sign.

The aggadah mentioned in *Midrash Tanhuma* thus represents a merger of folk views and of traditions whose source was the midrashim which sought to interpret the Biblical texts. This blend leads us to ask to what extent the aggadic literature is a folk literature, or, at least, to examine the question of the extent to which the folk element finds expression in the Midrash.

The common definition of folk literature is: "Literature which is transmitted orally from one generation to another by the entire society." This definition comprises three elements: oral transmission (excluding written means), continuity from generation to generation, and the participation of the entire society in this process. The absence of any one of the factors prevents the material from being defined as folk literature. If literature is transmitted orally from generation to generation without the entire society being involved in the transmission, it can be a special family tradition for a small circle of individuals. Literature transmitted orally by the entire society but not from one generation to the next, is literature which only has significance for one period of time (stories which were composed following a very striking event, etc.). The next generation sees no reason to repeat this literature, and thereby prevents it from becoming part of the literature of the entire social group. Literature which is transmitted from generation to generation by the entire society but without this being done orally is a frozen literature, such as the poems of a famous poet which are to be found on the bookshelves, and thus this passes from father to son. Only literature which realizes all three of the factors can thus be considered to be real folk literature. The existence of these factors is evidence of the fact that the nation, as a group, regards a certain literary unit to be part of its heritage and transmits it from father to son, from teacher to pupil, from generation to generation.

How do these three factors exist in regard to the literature of our Sages in general, and their aggadic literature in particular? As far as transmission orally is concerned, we can answer this easily. From many sources we learn that the literature of our Sages was created, transmitted and even implemented in most cases as an oral literature, by means of memory and word of mouth. "Those matters which are oral, you are forbidden to commit to writing," stated our Sages (*Gittin* 60b), and they thus expressed the clear difference between the written Torah (the Bible, which is to be read from a scroll or book), and the oral Torah, such as the Mishnah, which was to be studied orally. According to our Sages, God's will was revealed to His people in two parallel ways: in writing (and the Gentiles, too, have access to these writings) and orally (and this is only open to the Jewish people). This differentiation between the two was preserved for an extended period of time, and the Sages even stated that "one who writes the aggadah has no place in the World to Come" (Jerusalem Talmud, *Shabbat* 15:1). The prayer formulation, too, was transmitted orally until a late period. Those who translated the Torah into Aramaic in the synagogue were also required to do so from memory. The translator was forbidden to look in the Torah scroll, so that the differentiation between the written and oral Torahs would be stressed. Only at a later stage was the oral Torah permitted to be written down, because they were afraid it would be forgotten by the Jewish people given the vicissitudes of the times, and the Sages justified this step by claiming that (Ps. 119:126), "It is time for you, Lord, to work: for they voided Your Torah;" or, as they interpreted the verse, "It is time to work for the Lord, and void Your Torah."

From this, we see the great importance that our Sages stressed on going over the material, for "one who studies his material a hundred times is not the same as one who studies his material a hundred and one times" (*Hagigah* 9b), and that is not a gross exaggeration. We also know of the existence of the "*Tanna*," a person gifted with an unusual memory, who served our Sages as a walking text. Whenever there was a doubt about the exact language of a certain law, for example, the *Tanna* was summoned, and he gave the authoritative text by recalling it from his prodigious memory. In this regard, we must also mention the practice of our Sages to stress, whenever they quoted others, from whom they had heard the statement, and from whom he had heard it (along the lines of: "R' X stated in the name of R' Y in the name of R' Z," etc.). We have already seen in the previous chapter, in regard to the story of Hiel, that the story had already been told in the 3rd century C.E., but had for some reason not been committed to writing until the beginning of the Middle Ages. This story was evidently transmitted orally for many generations, until it was finally written down.

From here we can see that, as regards the first condition in the definition of folk literature, transmission orally, the literature of our Sages is — in the vast majority of cases — folk literature. Again, as regards the second condition, transmission from generation to generation, one can easily answer this affirmatively: the traditions that were created during the Tannaitic times, and even earlier, are repeated in the Amoraic times (and afterwards), as we saw often in the previous chapters. Incidentally, this transmission from generation to generation poses great obstacles to the scholar who wishes to place each tradition in its original historic setting, and yet, for example, finds in a 6th century work anonymous statements whose source may trace back to the 1st century C.E.

The third condition — transmission by the entire society — is more problematic. It is difficult to imagine that the masses, shepherds around the fire in Shefaram or Peki'in, or women who wove cloth in the markets of Tiberias or Zippori, spent their time quoting passages from the midrash and aggadah. The material found in the aggadic midrashim was, as a rule, transmitted by the Sages, *darshanim* and teachers, whose profession was study, and from that point of view the aggadah is not folk literature. But we must remember that the transmission of the Torah by the Sages was done *on behalf of* the entire society: it was not preserved in a closed and secluded esoteric framework, away from the eyes of all, but was offered to all the people by means of public sermons, the translation of the Torah into Aramaic, or education in school.

The aggadic literature of our Sages, if we summarize this section, is not a clearly folk literature. It does, indeed, answer to the first two conditions (oral transmission from generation to generation), but only answers partially to the third. We therefore must deal with the question which we posed in a different way, by isolating the folk elements in the literature of our Sages (and below we will indicate three of them: literary motifs, proverbs and folk tales). As opposed to the previous chapters, in which we spoke of literatures and cultures *outside* that of our Sages, we will focus below on passages *within* this literature, which reflect the cultural world of the masses, those who tilled the soil, craftsmen and petty traders, etc. These passages, too, have the power to contribute to our understanding of the world which surrounded the study hall and its literary works.

It is customary to regard literary motifs which occur among different cultural societies and which have been documented in many literatures around the world as folk motifs, which are the fruits of man's creativity wherever he may be. Comparative research of folk tales can thus give us one criterion, although not an exclusive one, to identify these motifs. A horn growing from a man's forehead, as mentioned above, is such a motif. Another folk motif is the belief that the blood of infant is an efficacious remedy for leprosy. According to the Midrash, Pharaoh became leprous and commanded cruelly that 150 Jewish infants be slaughtered each evening and morning so that he could bathe in their blood. A widespread and international motif is the tradition that the first human was born androgynous — half male and half female; this motif is repeated in the ancient Greek creation myths, as well as in India, among various South American tribes and others, and is to be found in the Midrash as well. Blood of a person who was killed which bubbles until the murder is avenged, earth that opens up and swallows up a person in distress, women who are hanged by their tongues for gossiping, regarding rain as teardrops from the heavens which are in mourning for having been detached from the earth — all these and many others are motifs which find expression in the works of many nations in general, and in the literature of our Sages in particular. It is therefore logical to assume that our Sages absorbed such motifs from the folk cultures and incorporated them in their literary works, as we saw above in reading the aggadah about Cain.

Another area of folk creativity that one can find in the literature of our Sages is the various proverbs which the Sages themselves admitted had been composed among the people. These proverbs are in most cases quoted in Aramaic, that being the language used by the masses, and we very often find them preceded by the phrase, "This is what people say." This formulation is the clearest possible evidence that this particular proverb was a common one in everyday use. We will bring three examples of such proverbs: a) "If you enter a city, follow its customs," which is the same as "When in Rome, do as the Romans do." b) A person bitten by a snake fears the rope" — "Once burned, twice shy," implying that a person who has had an unpleasant experience will be doubly — possibly excessively — cautious. c) "Poverty becomes a Jew as a red strap a white horse" — a very ironical statement, that poverty suits a Jew better than wealth. Proverbs such as these are brought by our Sages for various reasons: in order to explain a difficult Biblical verse, in order to encourage the listeners at a particularly trying time, etc.

More important to the topic at hand here are the stories which appear here and there in the literature of our Sages, which can be proven to have originated among the common folk. Here is an example of one of them (*Vayikra Rabbah* 12:1):

> A certain man sold all the goods in his house and used the proceeds to buy wine, which he drank. He sold the walls of his house and drank up the proceeds. His children complained and said: "This old man, our father, is going to leave the world and will leave us nothing after his death. What should we do to him? Let us get him drunk and take him out and claim that he died. We will then place him in his grave." And that is what they did: they took him and made him drunk and took him out and placed him in a certain cemetery.

In order to understand the story, we must remember that it is based on the practice that was current in Galilee at the time that the story was composed. There it was customary to bury people in caves and crypts. Thus the father who kept getting drunk was placed by his sons in a burial crypt, but was not buried in the ground. And the story goes on:

> A number of donkey drivers passed on their way to that city. They heard that a tax had suddenly been imposed on the province. They said: "Let us unload these jugs of wine in this cave and flee." That was what they did: They unloaded their goods within the cave and went to see what was happening in the city. Meanwhile, the old man was lying there, but when the donkey drivers saw him, they thought he was dead. When he awoke from his sleep, he saw a jug of wine above his head. He

unfastened it, put his mouth to it and began to drink. Once he
was sated, he began to sing. Three days later, the sons said: "Let
us go and see what our father is doing. Is he alive or dead?" They
came and found him, with a jug of wine at his mouth, and he
was sitting and drinking. They said to him: "If here, among the
dead, your Creator did not desert you, will He then desert you
among the living? As this was given you from the heavens, we
do not know what to do with you. Let us bring you back home
and we will set aside a fixed allotment for you." They set aside a
fixed allotment for him, and each of them would supply him
with drink for one of the days of the week.

One can prove — by studying the form, the language, and the
rhetorical basis of the story and on the basis of parallels in world
literature — that this is a folk story that was brought by our Sages in
the Midrash (possibly by changing its original ending). The story is
not exactly one with a moral message: it tells of a drunken father
who neglects his duties to his sons, and of sons who flagrantly
violate the law of "Honor your father." God's Providence comes to
the father's aid and helps him, without his being aware of the fact,
to overcome the obstacle posed him by his children. And it is
interesting to find that this story is brought in the Midrash in the
context of a lengthy diatribe against wine! After the *darshan* proves
that all of the evil in the world comes from the fruit of the vine (it
was because of it that Noah and Lot sinned, because of it the
Northern Kingdom was destroyed, etc.), he tells us this story in
order to balance the picture somewhat. Indeed, drunkenness is bad
and harmful, but when it stand in opposition to the value of
honoring one's parents, it is possible there are things that are worse
than it.

Below is another, humorous story, which has many parallels in
world literature. It deals with the relationship between Jews and
non-Jews (in this case: Jerusalemites and an Athenian), a favorite
topic of folk story tellers:

Four men from Jerusalem came to Athens and lodged with a
certain man. That evening, he made them a meal. After they had
eaten and drank, he prepared four beds for them. One of the

99

beds had a broken leg, and it was propped up against another. When they were ready to go to sleep, the householder said: "I have heard that the people of Jerusalem are very wise. I will listen to what they are talking about." He went in and lay down at their side. The guest who had been sleeping on the broken bed got up at night and said to his comrades: "Do you think that I have been lying on a bed? I am but suspended from the ground." One of his friends answered him: "The meat that we ate tasted of dog meat." The third said: "The wine that we ate drank was of the grave." The fourth said to them: "And are you surprised at all of these? The person with whom we are lodging is not his father's son." When the householder heard all these things, he said: "One of these statements (i.e., about the bed, of course) is true, and the others are false." He got up in the morning and went to the butcher. He said to him: "Give me of the meat that you sold me yesterday." He said to him: "I do not have any." He said to him: "What was it?" He said to him, "I had a tender young lamb, and when its mother died, we brought a female dog and it nursed the lamb." The householder said: "Two are the truth and two are false." He went to the one who sold the wine. He said to him: "Give me of the wine you sold me yesterday." He said to him: "I do not have any." He said to him: "What was it?" He said to him: "We have a single vine, planted on the grave of our father, and it gave us barely enough wine. When you came yesterday, we had no other wine, and we gave you of it." He said: "Three are true and one is false." He went to his mother and said to her: "Whose son am I?" She said to him: "You are the son of your father." He said to her: "Tell me the truth, or I will cut off your head!" She said to him: "My son, your father was unable to make me conceive, and I was afraid that his relatives would take all his possessions. I therefore committed adultery and brought you to this wealth and fame." The man said: "How is this, that the people of Jerusalem will come and make us illegitimate? We will make a decree that we will no longer host them" (*Ekhah Rabbah* 1).

Here too, the story was introduced into the midrash in an

interesting way. It appears in a midrash devoted to the destruction of the Second Temple and its horrors (*Ekhah Rabbah*). The midrash is essentially a description of the destruction of Jerusalem, the failure of the Bar Kokhba revolt, the terrible suffering endured by the Jewish people, its humiliation before the nations of the world, and similar topics. And within this context there suddenly appears a series of amusing stories, contrasting the Jews with the Athenians, citizens of the great city, the center of wisdom at that period. The purpose of the stories is to give heart to the wounded and stricken people, and to tell them that as long as they have a spiritual advantage over the Gentiles, they should not lose hope.

We will end with another story, one of the heroes of which is a well-known historical figure, King Herod Agrippas I. This story comes from *Vayikra Rabbah* (3:5), a midrash well-known for its affection for folktales:

> King Agrippas wanted to sacrifice one thousand burnt offerings on one day. He sent to the priest and said, "Let no one sacrifice today except me." A poor man came with two doves in his hands. He said to him [the priest], "Sacrifice these for me." [The priest] said to him, "The king commanded me and said 'Let no one sacrifice today except me'. [The poor man] said to him, "My Lord Priest, every day I catch four doves. I sacrifice two and make my living from two. If you do not sacrifice them, you are cutting into my living." So he took them and sacrificed them. It appeared to King Agrippas in a dream: A poor man's sacrifice came before yours. He sent for the priest and said, "Did I not say to you that no one should sacrifice today except me?" The priest said, "My Lord King, a poor man came to me with two doves and said to me ... 'My Lord Priest, I catch four doves every day. I sacrifice two and make my living from two. If you do not sacrifice them, you are cutting into my living.' Should I not have sacrificed them?" The king said to him, "All that you did, you did well."

The central point of the story is apparently the tension between the powerful king who wanted to sacrifice a thousand burnt offerings (of cattle) in one day, and the poor hunter who only

101

wished to sacrifice two doves. The victor in this conflict is the one the narrator wanted to win, the one with whom the audience could identify — in this case, the poor man. The great king with all his sacrifices does not attain the same religious rank as the poor man in his simple faith. King Agrippas is informed by heaven that the meager sacrifice of the poor man is preferred to his.

The story ends in an atmosphere of reconciliation. The king does not punish the poor man or the priest, but accepts the ruling and admits the justice of their actions. The way the king is depicted in the story is certainly very interesting. Other stories also tell us that Herod Agrippas I (who is evidently the hero of this story) was a popular king, and it is not, therefore, surprising that the people told stories of this kind about him. Folktales generally give innocent, unprejudiced information, and the one quoted above supplies us with a scrap of information about the favorable attitude of the masses to King Herod Agrippas, in his own time and at later periods.

The popular motifs, proverbs and folktales which appear in the literature of the Sages are proof that we are not dealing with a literature created in an ivory tower, cut off from the pulse of the people and its culture. The Sages lived among the people, and introduced the popular culture into their works, as we have already mentioned briefly in other contexts (see Chapters 6—7 above). This emerges not only in the ways we have discussed here, but also in the way they refer to superstitious beliefs, folk medicine prescriptions, methods of casting out demons, or of preventing a bridegroom from approaching his bride on their wedding night, stories of the powers of darkness and wicked angels, oaths and curses, and even obscenities and abuse, and other such matters.

IX.

Bible Translations and Liturgical Poetry

Throughout our survey we have concentrated on the nature of the various literatures and cultures surrounding the aggadic literature of the Sages, and which served as a background to it. In the previous chapter we began dealing with the literature of the Sages itself, in an attempt to discover the elements it drew from contemporary popular literature. In this chapter we will discuss two different literary genres produced in the study halls of the Sages, which can also serve as background to their aggadic literature: *targum* and *piyyut* (translation and poetry). Some people see these as an essential part of the literature of the Sages, but it is more usual to regard them as merely closely related to it.

The term *targum* refers, of course, to translations of the Bible into various languages, a phenomenon which originated as early as the third century B.C.E., very close to the time of the canonization of the Scriptures. The need for translations arose mainly when Hebrew ceased to be the spoken language of the people of Israel and its place was taken by foreign languages like Aramaic and Greek. The passage of time after the canonization of the Scriptures, which was marked by rapid political, social and cultural developments, also created the need to draw believers closer to the Scriptures by means of interpretation in a new light, one more appropriate to later generations. The earliest translation of the Bible was the Greek one known as the Septuagint. It includes all the books of the Bible, admittedly in an order different from the accepted one, as well as some apocryphal books (for details see Chapter 2 above). This translation, as far as we know, grew and consolidated in stages, with the Torah being translated as early as the third century B.C.E. One of the apocryphal books, the *Letter of Aristeas*, gives an account of this translation. According to this work, Ptolemy II, the king of Egypt, summoned seventy-two elders from Eretz Israel and, at his request, they translated the Torah into Greek within a few weeks. There is no need to accept this literary account as the historical truth, but it is evidently based on the obvious fact that the Septuagint originated among Jewish circles in Egypt in the early Hellenistic period (on this see Chapter 3 above). Many Egyptian Jews were already unfamiliar with Hebrew, and had to make do with this substitute. When Christianity arose on the stage of history, it adopted this translation as a sacred text (beside the New Testament, of course).

The Septuagint has a tendency to translate literally, as far as is possible in translating from Hebrew to Greek, but here and there deviations or expansions can be found in it which are relevant to a discussion of aggadic literature. (Nor should it be forgotten that this translation is also of very great importance because it reflects an ancient Hebrew version which is not identical in every detail to the text we know today.) For example, the Septuagint translates the verse "And Cain said to Abel, his brother" (*Genesis* 4:8), a puzzling verse which, in the version we have, does not tell us exactly what Cain said to his brother. Then the Septuagint puts into Cain's mouth the words: "Let us go out to the field." And indeed the story continues with the two in the field: "And it came to pass, when they were in the field, that Cain rose up against his brother, and slew him" (*ibid.* 9). This addition of "Let us go out to the field," if it did not appear in an early version of the Torah and was lost in the course of time, is an example of an aggadic element which found its way into the Septuagint.

In the Septuagint translation of the Psalms, for example, several psalms which are anonymous in our text (such as Psalms 61 or 93) are explicitly attributed to King David, while Psalm 144 is stated by the translation to be "against Goliath." This too apparently arises from an aggadic tradition well-known in the literature of the Sages that David was the author of the Psalms. The early translation reflected this tradition by the addition of titles to some psalms, and this proves its antiquity and its wide dispersion.

When the Septuagint speaks of the wife of Jeroboam, whom the Hebrew Bible does not bother to name (I Kings 14:5), it calls her Anno. This naming of anonymous Biblical figures is characteristic of aggadic literature in general, two examples being the name the Sages gave to Abraham's mother, Amthalai the daughter of Carabno, and to Lot's wife, Edith. The Septuagint, several hundreds of years earlier than the aggadic literature of the Sages, evidently already shows this tendency. The importance of this statement for research into the history of aggadic method is self-evident.

As well as the Septuagint, we also have other translations into Greek, such as the version of Aquila which will be mentioned below, and translations into other foreign languages. Of these, we will first mention the *Peshitta*, the Syriac version of the second or third century C.E. It is not clear whether this was produced in Jewish circles, or by Christians with the help of their Jewish brethren. The *Peshitta* is a literal version, lightly sprinkled with aggadah. Another important translation is the Vulgate, the Latin version produced in Eretz Israel in the fourth to fifth century by Jerome, one of the Church Fathers (who will be discussed later).

All the works that have been mentioned so far are far less important from our point of view than the large group of translations into Aramaic (*targumim*) which originated in circles close to those of the literature of the Sages. This is a relatively large group of texts, and we will mention only a few of them. The first of these, the most famous of all *targumim*, is the only one which is simply called *Targum* with no need for further precision or definition — the *Targum of Onkelos*. It includes only the Torah, and was well-known and widespread among the Jewish people in all its generations and diasporas.

The *Targum of Onkelos* seems to have originated in Eretz Israel, apparently in the Tannaic period, but was later given its final form in Babylon in the third or fourth century. The Babylonians greatly

105

The World of the Aggadah

valued this *targum*, and their successors, the Geonim of Babylon, continued to speak its praises and thus ensured its special status among the Jewish people. The production of this *targum* was ascribed to Onkelos, a proselyte among the pupils of R. Eliezer and R. Joshua of the first century, but scholars of *targum* believe that it was not Onkelos the proselyte who produced this translation. It is generally assumed that the name Onkelos is only a corruption of the Greek name Aquila, which was, as mentioned, the name of one of those who translated the Torah into Greek. According to this theory, the *targum*, the author of which was unknown, was ascribed to Aquila, and the name was then corrupted into Onkelos. All this was done out of the desire not to have to depend on an anonymous work.

Be that as it may, we have here an early translation of the whole Torah, the qualities of which can be described very precisely. Onkelos tends to translate the Hebrew original literally, almost word for word (apart from particularly difficult verses, where he offers paraphrases of what is said, and apart from the relatively rare cases where he translates a version different from that known to us). He diverges from the original Hebrew mainly in places where this serves his purposes. One of these purposes is to avoid anthropomorphism, that is to refrain from describing God in terms and concepts only appropriate to human beings. Almost always when the Torah mentions the "finger of God," or "His hand," and when it speaks of God's descending, or walking, or smelling, Onkelos avoids a literal translation and seeks a substitute. For example, where the Torah says "under His feet," referring to God (Exodus 24:10), he translates it as if it were "under His chair." When it says "And the Lord smelled a sweet savor" (Genesis 8:21), the phrase is translated very freely, as if it were "The Lord gladly accepted the sacrifice," all in order to avoid saying that God has feet, or possesses a sense of smell, like a man. When emotions (anger, sorrow etc.) are mentioned, Onkelos generally refrains from attributing them to God, and finds ways of getting around the reference to them in the Torah.

Another characteristic of this *targum* is the attempt to protect the reputation of the first patriarchs of the nation. Whenever Onkelos thinks a story contains the slightest possible hint at damage to the reputation of an admired character, he corrects it, softens it, or alters it completely. For example, when Isaac tells Esau that Jacob has taken his birthright from him "with subtlety" (Genesis 27:35), Onkelos translates it "with cleverness." When the Torah (Genesis 29:16) says that Leah's eyes were "weak," this is not intended as a compliment, as it was because of this defect that Jacob preferred Rachel to her sister. Onkelos translates "weak" as is if it were "beautiful." It is true that this creates a problem (for why, then, should Jacob prefer Rachel?), but he evidently preferred to do this than to say something uncomplimentary about one of the Matriarchs. Similarly, when the Torah says that "Rachel had stolen the idols" (Genesis 31:19), Onkelos translates it as "had taken," also in order to avoid speaking ill of Rachel.

Apart from these two tendencies, to protect the reputation of the Patriarchs of the nation and to avoid anthropomorphism, the *Targum of Onkelos* also contains some other additions and expansions of an aggadic nature, the inclusion of which cannot be easily explained. One example is his translation of "You shall rise up before the hoary head" (Leviticus 19:32). He translates this verse as if it is about standing up before a scholar (and not simply an elderly man). In this Onkelos is dependent on the Sages, who interpreted this verse by a play on words: "An old man is one who has acquired wisdom" (in Hebrew this is an acronym: an old man — *zaken*; one — *zeh*; has acquired — *kanah*).

Beside the *Targum of Onkelos*, we will also mention the *Targum Jonathan*, the translation by Jonathan ben Uziel of the books of the Prophets, a *targum* which is close in spirit and language to Onkelos. It can, therefore, be assumed that the two translators were contemporaries and from the same area.

Another *targum* of the Torah is the one printed in our Pentateuchs under the name *Targum Jonathan*, although it has been known for centuries that this attribution is mistaken. This is a Palestinian *targum* also known as the *Targum Yerushalmi* — the *Jerusalem Translation*. Note that the word *Yerushalmi* can also

107

mean "from Eretz Israel." For example, compare the *Talmud Yerushalmi* (the Jerusalem Talmud), which was not written in Jerusalem, despite its name! Someone abbreviated the title *Targum Yerushalmi* to its initials, T.Y., and someone else mistakenly interpreted these initials as those of *Targum Jonathan* (presumably he knew the *Targum Jonathan* on the Prophets).

Scholarship prefers, therefore, to call this *targum* the *Targum Pseudo-Jonathan*. It is also Eretz Israel in origin, but the question of its date is more complicated. On the one hand, some very early elements can be identified in it, such as a blessing for King John Hyrcanus (135—104 B.C.E.), the language of which shows that it was spoken in that king's lifetime. But on the other hand this *targum* also shows clear signs of lateness, such as the names it gives to Ishmael's wives: Ayesha and Fatima, names familiar to us from accounts of the life of Muhammad, the Prophet of Islam. The translator apparently wished to depict Ishmael as the ancestor of the Muslims, and therefore decided that his wives should bear the names of Muhammad's wife and daughter. The *Targum Pseudo-Jonathan* passed, therefore, through several transformations and the hands of several editors between the two dates given, the Hasmonean and the Islamic periods.

From the literary point of view and that of the method of translation it adopts, this *targum* is completely different from that of Onkelos. It contains what must certainly be thousands of additions to the Biblical text translated, some of them brief (a word or two) and some long and elaborate. Sometimes the verse is so broken down under the weight of the additions the translator piles on it, that it completely disappears. Many of these additions have no parallel in the literature of the Sages, and in many of them a clear folklore element is recognizable. For instance, the translator puts a bitter argument into the mouths of Cain and Abel before the murder. The brothers are debating complicated theological questions, and then Cain says (*Genesis* 4:8, freely translated):

I see that the world was created with mercy, but it is not conducted according to good actions. Favor is given in judgment; there is no judgment and no judge. Why was my

108

sacrifice not accepted with pleasure while yours was accepted with pleasure?

Abel answers, "There is judgment and there is a judge, and there is no favor" etc.

The appearance of a long and fully developed dialogue like this would be impossible in Onkelos, but there are many like it in the *Targum Pseudo-Jonathan.*

We also possess other Aramaic *targumim* both of the Torah and of the whole Bible, but this discussion of Onkelos and of the *Targum Pseudo-Jonathan* should be sufficient to represent this varied group. The basis of all these works is the custom, well-documented in the literature of the Sages, of translating the Torah into Aramaic, verse after verse, alongside the reading of the Torah in the synagogues on Sabbaths and festivals. The translator stood beside the reader of the Torah and they spoke alternately, so that the congregation heard every verse in the original accompanied by its translation or paraphrase in Aramaic. The translator's purpose was to assist his listeners to understand the sacred text. He performed this task primarily for those who did not know Hebrew, but he did not restrict himself merely to translating the Scriptures from one language to another, but adapted, expanded and explained it at every point where he thought this would be of use to the listeners. He therefore adopted the methods described above and others similar to them: avoidance of anthropomorphism, protection of the Patriarchs' reputation, blurring of contradictions found in the Torah, emphasis on the importance of certain commandments, avoidance of troublesome theological problems, etc. As far as we know, these translators were professionals who earned their living by this work, and were subjected to the continual supervision of the Sages, who checked that they did their work correctly and appropriately.

As I see it, the great importance for our subject of these translated texts is this: they enable us to see how the Sages (through the medium of the translations) presented their principal teachings to the people in the synagogues, and this assists us to reconstruct the socio-cultural atmosphere within which the Sages were active.

The World of the Aggadah

Needless to say, we will frequently find in the *targumim* an aggadic tradition which was not recorded anywhere else. The *targumim*, therefore, also serve as a reliable and valuable source for discovering aggadic traditions which arose within the circles of the Sages.

As well as the *targumim*, we should also mention another type of literature which also had its roots in the synagogue: *piyyut* (liturgical poetry). This is poetry intended to grace religious ceremonies, particularly public prayer, and even circumcision and wedding ceremonies, and other such. At a certain stage the regular public prayer apparently became a formal routine, in which it was difficult to make any innovation, and which was repeated over and over again, mechanically and in parrot fashion. This poetry was intended to provide a lyrical alternative to the formulaic prayers. This means that, as opposed to our modern custom of reciting the *piyyut* after the regular prayers, purely as an ornament, our forefathers would occasionally listen to a poet and fulfill their obligation of prayer in this way. The poet used to compose a new hymn for each occasion, in order to attract listeners and to satisfy their desire for new, fresh prayers. The poets drew their subject matter chiefly from the aggadic literature with which they were familiar, both in writing and orally. In its poetic form, its ways of expression and its function, liturgical poetry is, therefore, different from aggadic literature, but its content is extremely close to it, and this is what we will concentrate on in what follows.

As mentioned above (in Chapter 1), the first liturgical poets were from Eretz Israel. The first whom we know by name, from the fourth to the fifth century, was Yose ben Yose (who was apparently given this name because his father died before he was born). His *piyyutim* were lyrically very simple, and were chiefly *selihot* (prayers of repentance) or other hymns for the Days of Awe. One special type of *piyyut* composed by Yose ben Yose was the *Avodah* (worship). This was constructed as a long poem, describing in detail the order of worship performed by the priest in the Temple on *Yom Kippur*. As is well known, there is in the Mishnah a tractate named *Yoma*, which is almost entirely devoted to a description of the actions of the High Priest on Yom Kippur, and the poets who wrote

110

"worships" used to put its contents into poetic and lyrical form. But before the poet began describing the priest's actions, he usually narrated the history of the world from the Creation to the Exodus from Egypt and the building of the Temple. He evidently wished to say that the building of the Temple — and specifically the worship in it on Yom Kippur — were the high point of all history and that all events led up to it. Now in his account of the history of the world, the poet relied on many aggadic traditions, some of them known from the aggadic literature and some found only here. Thus the poet joins the long list of sources providing valuable information for the dating of traditions, since his time and place are known to us. For example, in telling the story of Jacob's ladder, he says:

The One who knows him stood above him in his sleeping place,
And said: I am your guard, a shadow on your right hand,
Holy Ones descend and ascend, for his sake,
To recognize his shape engraved on high.

The sense is this: God (here called "the One who knows him") came to Jacob in the place where he slept and promised to watch over his steps, like a shadow. The angels (the holy ones) go up and down the ladder in order to see Jacob, because his figure is engraved on the throne of God on High, and they yearn to see him in person. The tradition that the figure of Jacob was engraved on High, and that for its sake the angels came down to earth is an aggadic tradition which also appears in the midrashim.

Another poet, about a century later than Yose ben Yose, was called Yannai. He also lived in Eretz Israel, the motherland of *Piyyut*, and his poetry was more developed from a literary point of view than that of his predecessors. Yannai devoted most of his powers to writing *Kerovot*, which is the name given to a type of *piyyut* intended as an alternative to the central prayer of the Jewish people, the *Amidah*, also called the "Prayer of the Eighteen" (although in fact it contains nineteen benedictions on a weekday, and only seven on the Sabbath or a festival), or the "Silent Prayer." This prayer is said twice on every occasion (except for the evening prayer), once by every person praying individually (in a whisper) and once by the leader of the congregation. Yannai wanted the

111

congregation not to have to listen to the leader repeating the same formula time after time, so he composed a different version of this prayer for every Sabbath and every festival. In this he was greatly assisted by the aggadic traditions he knew. Nor did he hesitate to put *halakhic* material into poetry. As an example, we will give his words in the *Kerovah* which he wrote for one of the Sabbaths on which Leviticus was read from the Torah:

Indeed, for three transgressions
Women transgress and die in childbirth
For the sacred bread of the Sabbath;
For the candle of the Sabbath;
For the period of purification,
For she has not maintained it in holiness...

Now compare what is written in the Mishnah: "There are three transgressions for which women die in childbirth: for not taking care over purification, over the Sabbath bread, and over lighting the Sabbath candle" (*Shabbat* 2:6).

Yannai's words are frequently unparalleled in the aggadic literature of the Sages. Did he know a tradition which we have already lost, or did he invent these himself? For example, he says of the rod which Aaron threw down before Pharaoh: "He threw it down, and it became three kinds: A viper, a crocodile and a cobra."

We know of no other source which says that Aaron's rod actually turned into three reptiles.

We could continue to cite other poets, some well-known, like Eleazar b. R' Kalir, others less famous, like Joseph b. R' Nissim, Mevorakh ben Nathan, or Shimon b. R' Megas, whose works are embedded in the prayer books of various Jewish congregations, or found in many manuscripts. The famous Cairo Genizah, discovered less than a century ago, has revealed to us the names and the works of dozens of poets, an indication of the great demand there was for this kind of literature.

This fertile poetic literature is very important evidence for the existence of aggadic traditions and their dispersion. We are still waiting for a comprehensive study to assess the contribution of liturgical poetry to research on the aggadic literature of the Sages.

Meanwhile, the very fact that these poets were to be found in the social and literary circles surrounding the Sages is sufficient to suggest that anyone who wants to understand the world of the Sages in its entirety must include the liturgical poets in it. It should not be forgotten that it is possible that some of the sages also turned their hand to the art of poetry (just as they contributed much to the various regular prayers), and if this is the case, it is certainly quite impossible to separate liturgical poetry from aggadic literature.

X.

Halakhic Literature

At this stage in our survey, which is advancing from the remote to the close at hand, we have now reached the very heart of the literature of the Sages, texts which certainly originated in their study-halls and circles. Those who give a wider definition to the literature of the Sages will include in it the *siddur* — prayerbook — *targumim* and *piyyutim* (see previous chapter), but even those who prefer to define its scope more narrowly will admit that it has at least two branches, aggadah and halakhah (we discussed the definition and meaning of these terms in the first chapter).

The essay by Bialik with which this book began is likely to give the impression that aggadah and halakhah are two contrasting worlds, polar opposites for which it is impossible to find any common denominator or any correspondence. Bialik writes:

Halakhah has a stern countenance, aggadah has a cheerful countenance. The former is demanding, stringent, as hard as iron, the quality of strict justice; the latter is forgiving, lenient, as smooth as oil, the quality of mercy ... On the one hand, petrifying observance, obligation, servitude ... and on the other, constant renewal, freedom, liberty ... On the one hand — the dryness of prose, a firm and fixed style, gray, monotonous language, the rule of the intellect. And on the other hand — the vitality of poetry, a flowing, changing style, multi-hued language, the rule of the emotion.

It should be remembered that Bialik painted this clear-cut picture

114

not for its own sake, out of a study of the literature of the Sages, but as an introduction to a philosophical essay of contemporary application, dealing chiefly with the problems of his own generation, and it is worth our while to examine it carefully. We will therefore first indicate some elements common to both aggadah and halakhah, and then some of the differences between the two, and the relationship created when the two are brought together. First, one must emphasize that, in the study-halls, the same Sages dealt with both halakhah and aggadah. The student of the literature of the Sages will find the same names, such as R. Akiva, R. Yohanan and R. Pappa, recurring in both aggadic and halakhic sources and contexts. Occasionally, we will even find aggadah and halakhah discussed together in the same breath, as in the story of the Tanna, R. Meir, of whom it is said that every sermon he preached was one-third halakhah, one-third aggadah and one-third parables. The following story from the Babylonian Talmud also bears witness to a combination of this kind:

> R. Ami and R. Asi sat before R. Yitzhak Naphha. One said to him: "Tell us, master, words of halakhah," and the other said: "Tell us, master, words of aggadah." He began speaking words of aggadah, and the one did not permit him. He began speaking words of halakhah and the other did not permit him. He said to them: "I will tell you a parable: What does this resemble? A man who had two wives, one young and one old. The young one pulled out his white hairs [so that he would look young] and the other one pulled out his black hairs. In the end he became completely bald. Let me then tell you something that will suit both of you" (*Bava Kama* 60b).

He continues by preaching on a verse from the Torah, a sermon made up of a combination of halakhah (basically a halakhic pronouncement from the Biblical verse) and of aggadic material (which involves messianic consolation).

Only very rarely, in a small percentage of cases, do we find a sage who restricts his activity to one of the two fields. It appears that one of these was R. Eleazar ha-Modai, under whose name we have almost no halakhic material, although his knowledge of aggadah was so great that it became a custom that when people ran into difficulties over a complicated aggadic question, they would say: "We still need Ha-Modai," that is, "We are still waiting for R. Eleazar to come and explain the problem to us." But, as mentioned, this was an unusual case, the exception that proved the rule.

A similar story is told of R. Akiva and the way he dealt with the verse of Exodus 8:6:

"And the frogs came up and covered the land of Egypt." From a linguistic point of view the word *tzfardea* [frog in modern Hebrew] is in this verse a collective noun and, of course, does not only refer to a single frog, but R. Akiva decided to explain the use of the single form thus: "There was one frog, which swarmed and covered the whole land of Egypt."

According to this view, the story tells of one creature which multiplied in a remarkable and miraculous way. One of R. Akiva's contemporaries, R. Eleazar ben Azariah, reacted to this statement by saying: "Akiva, what have you got to do with aggadah? Finish what you have got to say and go and deal with plagues and issues of uncleanness"; that is to say, stop talking about aggadic matters and go and deal with questions of plagues and the various rulings on impurity, both of which are clearly halakhic questions. R. Eleazar went on to suggest his own interpretation of the verse: "There was one frog, which whistled to them [the rest of the frogs] and they came" (*Shemot Rabbah* 10:4). This story shows clearly that the Sages sometimes thought that there were people who were stronger in one field than the other. Usually, though, as mentioned, they dealt with both fields side by side.

The texts which have reached us from the literature of the Sages also combine aggadah with halakhah. Works which are usually considered purely halakhic include aggadic elements, sometimes fairly extensive ones. One example of this is the basic book of halakhic literature, the Mishnah, on which, of course, were constructed the Babylonian and Jerusalem Talmuds. The Mishnah includes not only an entire tractate which is entirely aggadic (Tractate *Avot*), but also much aggadic material scattered through various halakhic contexts, like the ending of Tractate *Ta'anit*:

There were no better days for Israel than the fifteenth of Av and Yom Kippur, when the daughters of Jerusalem went out in borrowed white dresses, so as not to shame those who had none... and the daughters of Jerusalem went out and danced in the vineyards. And what did they say? "Young man, lift up your eyes and see what you will choose for yourself. Do not turn your eyes to beauty; turn your eyes to the family..."

The stories of Samson who had his eyes gouged out as an appropriate punishment for having followed his eyes (in marrying Philistine women) and of Absalom, who prided himself on his hair and for that reason was hanged by it, are told in the Mishnah (Tractate *Sotah*) in a discussion of the laws on an adulteress, and there are many other examples. On the other hand a discussion on various halakhic matters can be found in what are clearly aggadic contexts, such as a discussion of questions of ritual slaughter while expounding the story of the sacrifice of Isaac, or an exposition on the permission to employ a Gentile wet nurse in a discussion of the story of finding of Moses in the Nile by Pharaoh's daughter. We also know of a particular type of public sermon in which the preacher used to preface his aggadic narrative with a question of halakhah (such as: "May our master teach us: what is the law about running on the Sabbath?" i.e. is it permitted to run on the Sabbath?, etc.). It is therefore impossible to make a clear-cut distinction between aggadic and halakhic texts, just as it is difficult to distinguish between sages who dealt with one or the other.

What is more, the qualification of a sage at that time included both aggadah and halakhah. For example, we are told of the founder of the center at Yavneh (Jamnia), R. Yohanan ben Zakkai that "he neglected neither the Bible, nor the Mishnah, nor the Gemara, nor the halakhah, nor the aggadah" (*Sukkah* 28a). The curriculum of the time demanded that the sage should be versed not only in the halakhic side of the Oral Torah, but also in the aggadic side.

In addition to everything said so far, it should be stressed that, when all is said and done, the subjects covered by aggadah and halakhah were identical. The purpose of the debate and its character were different, but the subjects concerned in it did not change:

117

Sabbaths and festivals, prayer and kashrut, the relations between Israel and the nations, and between the individual and his neighbors, the position of women, the education of children, and similar topics.

Finally, one must consider the methods of teaching halakhah and aggadah. In order to extract from Biblical verses everything that could possibly be learned out of them, the Sages developed special techniques, which they called *middot* (rules). They even left us a list of *middot* like these. One of them, for example, was the *middah* of *kal vahomer* (*a fortiori*, a *middah* which maintains: "if A, which is a relatively easy and simple matter, should be treated in this or that way, then B, which is a much more serious matter than A, should clearly be treated at least in the same way.") This is one of the thirteen *middot* employed in the halakhah and ascribed to R. Ishmael, as well as one of the thirty-two *middot* employed in the aggadah. Another *middah* is that of *gezerah shavah* (analogy), according to which one can deduce something new from the very fact that two different verses contain the same word. This *middah* is also employed in both aggadah and halakhah.

It should be stressed that if the same people worked on both halakhah and aggadah, if the same texts include both types, if the same subjects are discussed in both, and if this is done in the same ways in both, it is obvious that the distinction between the two cannot be clear-cut and well-defined. Moreover, it is apparently possible to indicate a real, internal interrelationship between these two aspects of the Oral Torah.

The aggadic rule: "An Israelite, even if he has sinned, is still an Israelite" (which means that a Jew who sins, even if the sin is apostasy, is still regarded as a Jew) served, admittedly for the most part after the period of the Sages, as the basis and foundation for a discussion of the question of the relations between an apostate Jew and his family who did not renounce their faith: should he give his wife a divorce? Should he have to release his dead brother's wife? Can he inherit his father's property, or leave his own to his sons? The aggadic rule cited above was applied to these questions and others, and the various halakhot were determined in its light.

118

25

A more complicated, but no less interesting example, pointed out by E. E. Urbach in an article discussing the relationship between halakhah and aggadah, is the question of the history of Jewish laws of inheritance. According to the Torah, the dead father's estate passes to his sons, and if they are no longer alive to his grandsons, and so on. Daughters do not inherit their father's estate, unless they have no brothers and they are married to members of the same tribe. Property that has been sold has to be redeemed and not left in the possession of the purchaser, etc. That is to say, there is a clear intention to keep the property within the family and not to allow it to pass to other ownership and to be held under another name. Now anyone who reads the literature of the Sages (and to a considerable extent the student of the halakhah as it is usually conducted today as well) will easily become aware of the difference between the Sages' laws of inheritance and those of the Torah. From the Sages time onwards daughters can inherit from their fathers unconditionally. The father can disinherit his sons and leave his property as a gift to whomsoever he wishes, while the duty to redeem property that has been sold to others gradually fades away and disappears. What this means is that the requirement to keep the property, the land and the buildings, within the family unit was abolished.

What caused this change? Why was the law of the Torah altered in the following generations? Various sociological or economic reasons were certainly contributory factors but, in Urbach's opinion, the change arose mainly out of developments which took place over a clearly aggadic issue, the question of the teachings on a man's reward and his fate after death. According to the Bible, man's reward comes in this world: "Honor your father and mother... that your days may be long in this land." A man is punished for his deeds — or rewarded for them — while he still lives and breathes, while after his death he passes from this world into a vague, immaterial way of being in which there is no question of reward or punishment, and no definite existence. The laws of inheritance are intended to ensure that the dead will not vanish, that his name will not be erased, and that his memory will be preserved among his family and on his land. This is the reason for the great importance that the Torah attaches to levirate, for example, as it ensures that the dead man's name will arise again on his estate (compare what it states in Ruth 4). The property he leaves in this world is the memorial and the symbol of the continued existence of the dead. Now, by the period of the Sages, a complete belief in a full life in the world to come had already developed (the questions of the origins of this belief, its nature and the factors that gave rise to it still need further clarification). From this time onwards reward and punishment were transferred to the other world, to heaven and hell. The dead no longer vanishes in the realm of oblivion, but continues his almost complete existence somewhere else. So the Sages interpret the words "that your days may be long" as referring to a longer life in a world which is completely good: In this view the connection between a man and his worldly property is gradually weakened. When man passes from one form of existence to another and continues to function in his new situation, he does not entirely disappear, and there is therefore no need to immortalize him in this world. That is to say, the transition which took place in halakhah from the Biblical law to the law formulated by the Sages arose from changes which took place on the plane of belief and aggadic concepts, and thus clearly reflects the internal interrelationship between halakhah and aggadah.

Despite everything that has been said so far, there are also a number of differences between halakhah and aggadah which should be indicated. First let us mention the obvious and almost self-evident fact that halakhah, in contrast to aggadah, has prescriptive force in real life. Halakhah is determined through the application of a complicated system of considerations, sometimes accepting a majority view and rejecting an individual opinion, sometimes considering decisive the opinions of the earliest generations and ignoring the arguments of later generations, etc. But once the halakhah was established, everyone who accepted its yoke had to obey it unquestioningly. Aggadah, on the other hand, was not binding in the same way, and the Sages said: "The man of the aggadah does not command and does not permit, does not make unclean and does not purify"; "We do not learn from the aggadah [halakhic matters]"; "One does not teach from the aggadah," etc. Everyone could relate to it as he wished and there was no framework that could compel him to adopt it or act according to it.

Another difference between aggadah and halakhah is expressed in the question of the importance of the duty to pass on a saying together with the name of its originator. As we have noted, in the literature of the Sages long chains of transmission sometimes appear before a certain saying (in the form: R' A said in the name of R' B, in the name of R' C, etc.). The need for these chains of transmission arises from the assumption that "no court can revoke the judgement of a fellow court, unless it is greater in both learning and in numbers," and on the basis of the feeling — which we will discuss later — that the first generations were of greater importance than those that followed them. If this was the case, one had to be very certain who were the first authors of a halakhic saying, for on this the validity or the compulsion to accept it often rested. But in the realm of aggadah this duty was not so strictly observed. "Copyright" is a modern concept. A sage who heard from another a pleasant story, a neat parable, or a witty proverb could repeat it on other occasions without having to apologize for using someone else's words, and without having to admit when or from whom he had heard it. The Torah was given in the desert, said the Sages, because that was the place of freedom, and the Torah is freely available to anyone who wants it.

Moreover, as we have already said, there is in halakhah a keen sense of a decline down through the generations (a sense which has evidently not disappeared even today). Every generation sees itself as inferior to the preceding one. "Better is the fingernail of the first ones than the belly of the last," said the Sages, and "If the first ones were the sons of angels, we are the sons of men. If the first ones were the sons of men, we are like asses" (*Shabbat* 114b). The generations are continually declining, and no generation has the right to challenge its predecessors. For this reason, nowhere in the halakhah does someone openly and directly contradict his predecessors. At most he will try to interpret their words in a way that seems

121

appropriate to him, but he will never say outright or openly that they were mistaken or confused. In aggadah, though, there is usually no such sense of decline. What is more, members of later generations did not hesitate to contradict their predecessors. The second century Tanna, R. Akiva, for example, said that the generation which died in the desert will not arise at the resurrection of the dead. Yet R. Yohanan of the third century explicitly contradicted him, saying: "R. Akiva abandoned his piety," and went on to give an opposing opinion. In the same way, four generations after the School of Hillel and the School of Shammai argued over the question of which was created first, the heavens or the earth, R. Simeon said, "I wonder how the fathers of the world could argue over this matter," and gave his own opinion, that the heavens and the earth were created at the same time, "like a pan and its lid."

It is obvious from all this that no need was felt in the field of aggadah to reach binding verdicts. Aggadah does not depend on a quorum in order to indicate or determine by a majority vote who is in the right. Contradictory views on aggadah can exist side by side, while the halakhic framework can, of course, not accept contradictions or uncertainties. There everything must be decided in one way or another. For example, there is an aggadic controversy over the exact date on which Moses was cast into the Nile. Some people say it was the sixth of Sivan (i.e. the same day on which the Torah was later given), while others say it was the twenty-first of Nissan (i.e. the day of the crossing of the Sea of Reeds, the seventh day of Passover). The sources present these two views side by side and, since they have no practical halakhic application, there is no need to decide between them, and so they were both preserved.

The same is true of many other aggadic issues. The rules for accepting proselytes are clear and unequivocal, but the aggadic questions of the nature and importance of the proselyte were not settled. On the one hand, there are some sayings like: "proselytes are as bad for Israel as a plague," but on the other hand some voices are heard saying that "Israel was exiled among the nations so that proselytes should be added it." The same is true of the question of attitudes to the Gentile. On the one hand, it is said: "The Gentile who converts and studies Torah is like the high priest," and on the other hand people said: "The best among the Gentiles should be killed."

This last saying needs a little clarification, particularly in the light of the use made of it in various contexts in recent times. It originated in a Tannaitic midrash to Exodus, the *Mekhilta*, and there it appears in the context of the pursuit of the Israelites by Pharaoh and the Egyptians with their six hundred chariots. The midrash asks:

Whose were the animals? Can you say that they were the Egyptians?... [for it had already been said, among the plagues of Egypt] "and all the cattle of Egypt died," or can you say that they were the Israelites?... [for Moses said] "our cattle also will go with us"... then whose were they?

The answer of the midrash is that the animals mentioned belonged to Egyptians who had feared the word of the Lord and had taken their beasts into their houses, when Moses had warned them of the plague of hail. So R. Shimon ben Yohai said: "the best among the Gentiles should be killed, and the best among the snakes should have its head crushed," since it was in fact the God-fearing Egyptians who impeded the Israelites. Many scholars and commentators struggled with this saying. Some corrected it and said: "the best among the Gentiles should be killed in time of war." Others interpreted it in a complicated way [by changing the Hebrew vowel sound] to imply "the best among the Gentiles is the dead one," without any command to do the killing. But there is obviously no need for the two interpretations, which have an excessively apologetic tone. R. Simeon ben Yohai, who lived around the time of the Bar Kokhba revolt and suffered terribly at the hands of the Romans, expressed an extreme opinion, but an opinion which is to be accepted no more nor less than any other. No authoritative body ever assembled to pronounce R. Simeon ben Yohai's saying accepted halakhah, which every Jew was required to obey. It is only one personal opinion, which can be set against others which are clearly opposed to it.

Moreover, the same sage was permitted to contradict himself over aggadah, and to change his mind without being criticized for it.

123

If he had done that in a halakhic context, there would immediately have been a great outcry, and demands for an explanation how the sage could contradict himself, and whether there was any way of reconciling his differing views. In cases of aggadah such a phenomenon was passed over as almost routine.

From everything said so far, it is obvious that in halakhah there was a clear development and stratification, layer after layer, in which every generation saw itself as the successor of the previous one, explaining or expanding what it had said. In aggadah we do not have development of this kind in most cases, but usually only uncontrolled growth and expansion. It is generally impossible to trace the line of development in an aggadic topic, since every generation could hold opposing views, and every generation could return to views heard in the past. It is almost impossible to trace in questions of aggadah the same structure of question and answer growing ever more elaborate from generation to generation that is found in halakhah.

One additional point: the discussion of halakhah was basically something restricted to the sages sitting on the benches in the study-halls, who gathered among themselves to clarify halakhic questions, some of them purely theoretical and floating in the air. Discussion of aggadah, on the other hand, was also intended for the masses. A story about this has been preserved in the Babylonian Talmud (*Sotah* 40a):

> R. Abahu and R. Hiyya happened to be together in one place. R. Abahu preached on aggadah and R. Hiyya preached on halakhah. Everyone left R. Hiyya and went to R. Abahu. R. Hiyya was upset. R. Abahu said to him, "I will relate a parable to you: What does this resemble? Two men, one selling precious stones and one selling all kinds of tinsel. To whom does the crowd rush? Is it not to the one selling tinsel?"

R. Abahu meant to say that halakhah is like a gem. One does not buy a diamond every day. One does so only on special occasions, after much preparation. But tinsel, cheap toys and other items worth only a few cents are bought on the spur of the moment, without any sense of the importance of the occasion. That is aggadah, says R. Abahu, which is not as valuable as halakhah, but which everyone can understand: popular, folk material. Perhaps R. Abahu only said this in order to comfort his friend, but in this way he evidently revealed his opinion of the relative value of halakhah and aggadah and their respective audiences.

Finally, the question of style. Bialik put it very well: aggadah has "the vitality of poetry, a flowing, changing style, multi-hued language, the rule of the emotion," while halakhah has "the dryness of prose, a firm and fixed style, gray, monotonous language, the rule of the intellect." This difference in style is, of course, derived from the great difference in essence between the two. Halakhah is a serious world, a matter of life and death, while there is a considerable element of playfulness in aggadah, amusement and light-heartedness. It is impossible to deal with both within the same linguistic framework.

To sum up: halakhah and aggadah are two different entities which comprise, between them, the literary and historical complex called the literature of the Sages. Like the Roman god, Janus, who is depicted with two faces, halakhah and aggadah, interconnected in their roots and their foundations, represent the different sides of the same entity. Through their contrasting concepts emerges an elaborate picture of an variegated and multi-faceted world.

XI.

Early Christian Literature

A complete survey of the literary and cultural world within which the literature of the Sages was created and employed necessarily involves some attention to the non-Jewish literatures with which the Sages came into contact, primarily early Christian, Samaritan and Islamic literature, and the last chapters of this book will be devoted to these three. We will begin with Christianity.

A considerable number of early Christians saw themselves for a very long time as part of the people of Israel, faithful to its Torah and its God. They saw their messiah as continuing the work of the Giver of the Torah, Moses, and of the greatest prophets. For this reason they were able, without great difficulty, to continue to conduct their lives within the framework of normal Jewish society of the time. There was not, for example, much difference between the everyday way of life and of observing the commandments of those who believed in Jesus as the messiah and of those who rejected him. The Jewish leaders of those generations saw this sort of coexistence as an internal threat and did everything they could to expel the Christians from their midst, for example by re-formulating the "benediction concerning sects," the twelfth benediction of the *Amidah* prayer, in which day after day they cursed their enemies and prayed for their destruction. In the Yavneh period (the end of the first century C.E.), at the time when the new faith began to gather strength and believers, it was decided to include the Judeo-Christians and Christians among those against

126

whom the curse was directed.

Some of the early Eretz Israel versions of this prayer specifically mention the Christians as those whose destruction and extermination are implored. At the same time, the process of separation between Christianity and Judaism was a long and complicated one, and it can reasonably be assumed that throughout the first two centuries C.E. Jews and Christians lived together in various forms of co-operation and coexistence. The two faiths were both persecuted by the Roman authorities, and this also assisted them to live together in one way or another as close neighbors.

The final break between the mother faith — Judaism — and its daughter — Christianity — apparently came at the beginning of the fourth century C.E. when, from being a persecuted belief, Christianity became the official religion of the Roman Empire. From this time onwards the two stood in direct and conscious opposition to each other, while Christianity exploited the new position of political power it had acquired in order to persecute Judaism with all its strength.

It is, therefore, not surprising that there should be two different aspects to the literary and ideological interrelations between Judaism and early Christianity: a. those which early Christianity borrowed from Judaism at the time when the two lived cheek by jowl, out of an understandable desire to emphasize the new faith's links with Judaism and it claim to being the legitimate successor to the Torah of Moses; b. the works of controversy and polemic produced by both sides when they wished to demonstrate the differences and contrasts between the two religions as clearly as possible. It is of course impossible to draw too sharp a line between the two tendencies, and they can sometimes stand indiscriminately side by side. (Nevertheless, I do not think that one can demonstrate the existence of a third possibility, of a genuine borrowing by Judaism from early Christianity. The Sages would certainly not have lent a hand to Christian propaganda by adopting the principles and teachings of a religion which claimed that it had its roots in Judaism. Later, in the Middle Ages, when the break between Judaism and Christianity was a clear-cut, decided issue, it was possible for a process of this kind to take place, but it is difficult to assume its existence in the period with which we are concerned.)

In surveying early Christian literature one should begin with a discussion of the basic book of the Christian Church, the New Testament. As noted, the Christians accepted the twenty-four books of the Jewish Bible, which, with the addition of some apocryphal books (see Chapter 2 above), they call the Old Testament. They added to these the books which comprise their New Testament, and thus they formed their own collection of sacred scriptures. There are twenty-seven books in the New Testament, written roughly between the years 70—150 C.E. This is an extremely short period of time, particularly in comparison with the many hundreds of years which passed between the beginning of the composition of the Jewish Bible and its completion. It is also very close in time to the events and the people with which it deals. Most of the books of the New Testament were written originally in Greek, the cultural language of the time, but some of them were apparently translated into that language from Hebrew or Aramaic, since a substrate of Semitic vocabulary and syntax can be detected beneath the Greek linguistic surface. Incidentally, there are also Christian "apocrypha," works which for various reasons were not accepted into its canon.

The New Testament includes thirteen epistles written by Paul, or written by others and attributed to him. Paul (or, to give him his Hebrew name, Saul) was a Jew who grew up in a Hellenistic cultural environment, was baptized as a Christian, and became one of those who fashioned the image and the teachings of the new religion. Some people claim that his contribution to shaping Christianity and disconnecting it from Judaism was greater than that of Jesus, the originator of the religion, who is considered its messiah. It is possible that without Paul's activities Christianity would have passed into the realm of oblivion, as happened to the Dead Sea Sect, for example, or to other sects which cut themselves off from the people of Israel and were forgotten by it. Paul's epistles (a literary form not found among the literature of the Sages) are addressed to the founders of the Christian faith and to new

Christian communities throughout the Roman Empire. They include many exhortations to believers in the new faith, and in these the theoretical and theological foundations of that faith are laid down, its messianic concepts and its attitudes to the Torah of Israel and its commandments. Among other things Paul makes much use of Biblical quotations in order to strengthen his claims, for example:

> For it is written that Abraham had two sons, the one by a bondmaid, the other by a freewoman. But he who was of the bondwoman [Ishmael] was born after the flesh, but he of the freewoman [Isaac] was by promise...

He goes on to compare Ishmael to the Covenant of Sinai, the first covenant pledged between God and His people, and Isaac to the new covenant pledged by means of Jesus, and continues:

> But as then he that was born after the flesh persecuted him that was born after the spirit, even so it is now. Nevertheless, what says the scripture? Cast out the bondwoman and her son: for the son of the bondwoman will not be heir with the son of the freewoman (Epistle to the Galatians 4:22—30).

In these last words an echo can be found of the common post-Biblical Jewish tradition of the enmity between Ishmael and Isaac (which is taken as a symbol of the relations between Israel and the Gentiles) as well as a method of relying on Biblical verses similar to that of the Sages, who were accustomed to prove their statements by quotations from the Bible prefaced by such phrases as "For it is said that...," or "For it is written that..." (Incidentally, Paul's quotation of this verse is far from accurate, see Genesis 21:10.) Scholars of the New Testament frequently mention the midrashic elements which appear in it, and one should not be surprised by this, since Saul/Paul was a Jew, and so were many of those he addressed, and they had all been educated in Jewish ways of studying the Bible.

More important for our purposes are three other works known as "gospels" (or "evangelia"), the Gospels of Matthew, of Mark and of Luke. These books contain three versions, sometimes identical, sometimes contradictory, of the life of Jesus, his sayings, his crucifixion and his resurrection from the dead. The comparison of these gospels, in an attempt to discover their common literary tradition and the historical truth lying behind them, is one of the most prolific fields of research into the New Testament. The three gospels were written within a period of about thirty years (usually accepted as being about 68 to 95 C.E.), and express different conceptions of the activities of Jesus, the events of his life and his personality, and this only one or two generations after he lived. The Gospel according to Matthew, which was written about 85 C.E., is considered, from a comparison with the other gospels, to be the closest in spirit and in concept to Judaism, to the extent that instructive examples can be taken from it of the way early Christianity borrowed from Judaism.

Here is the story of the birth of Jesus as it appears in Matthew 2:1—16:

> Now when Jesus was born in Bethlehem of Judea in the days of Herod the king, behold, there came wise men from the East to Jerusalem, saying, Where is he that is born King of the Jews? for we have seen his star in the east, and are come to worship him. When Herod the king had heard these things, he was troubled, and all Jerusalem with him. And when he had gathered all the chief priests and scribes of the people together, he demanded of them where [the messiah] should be born. And they said unto him: In Bethlehem of Judea [This is supported by the quotation of verses from the Bible] ... Then Herod, when he had privily called the wise men, enquired of them diligently what time the star appeared... The angel of the Lord appeared to Joseph [the husband of Mary, the mother of Jesus] in a dream, saying, Arise, and take the young child and his mother, and flee into Egypt... Then Herod... sent forth and slew all the children that were in Bethlehem, and in all the coasts thereof, from two years old and under, according to the time which he had diligently enquired of the wise men.

The story told here is remarkably similar to midrashic traditions of the birth of Moses in Egypt, such as the story in midrash *Shemot Rabbah*: the star-gazers, Pharaoh's priests, know beforehand of Moses' birth and of his destiny as his people's redeemer, and they

130

warn the king about him. On Moses' birth the house is filled with light, and thus the importance of the child is announced to the world; Pharaoh, the king, who fears for his throne, orders all the Israelite children to be put to death, in the belief that thus he will destroy Moses and cancel the prophecy of his priests; God helps the baby to be saved and does not allow him to fall into the hands of those who are seeking his life, etc. All these are literary motifs which frequently recur in the midrashim about Moses (and about other sacred figures, like Abraham), and it is quite clear that the Christian author deliberately transferred to his messianic hero stories he had heard about Moses at some time or other. By doing this, Matthew evidently intended to represent Jesus as a kind of "second Moses," the bringer of a new Torah, as opposed to the one who brought the old Torah. He expressed this concept by constructing a story about the birth of Jesus on the familiar model of the story of the birth of Moses. Needless to say, if one reads between the lines, this is also clear evidence that midrashic traditions on the birth of Moses were already widespread by the first century C.E., although most of them are documented only in later sources.

In another place, Matthew says that Jesus compared his generation with the people of Nineveh, saying: "The men of Nineveh will rise in judgment with this generation, and will condemn it; because they repented at the preaching of Jonah" (Matthew 12:41). That is to say, Jesus' generation will not be found innocent in its trial, for the people of Nineveh will bear witness against it by their deeds and will bring about its condemnation, for they repented and listened to the call of the prophet, while Jesus' generation refused to listen to the call of its prophet and even despised him. Now precisely this idea also occurs in the Midrash, *Ekhah Rabbah*, in the words of chastisement with which the preacher (in the name of God) upbraids Jerusalem:

And had she not to learn from the city of Jonah, from Nineveh? I sent one prophet to Nineveh and brought them to repentance, while as for Israel and Jerusalem, how many prophets have I sent them [and they have not repented]? (Introduction, 32).

131

It is a very probable assumption that here Jesus adapted for his own purposes, in the spirit of his beliefs and against the background of his life experiences, an early Jewish idea which contrasted Nineveh and Jerusalem — and not to the latter's advantage.

One of the most famous sections of the New Testament is what is known as the "Sermon on the Mount" (Matthew 5—7), a sermon preached by Jesus, large parts of which sound like a Pharisaic-Jewish text closely corresponding to the teachings of the Sages. Someone who reads this sermon without knowing its source would in most cases find it difficult to point to any real differences between its teachings and what he believes are the doctrines of the Sages. Here are three quotations from it:

a) Be you therefore perfect, as your Father which is in heaven is perfect. (5:48)

b) Take therefore no thought for the morrow: for the morrow will take thought for the things of itself; sufficient unto the day is the evil thereof. (6:34)

c) You hypocrite, first cast out the beam out of your own eye: and then shall you see clearly to cast out the mote out of your brother's eye. (7:5)

Compare these words with the following sayings of the Sages:

Just as He is merciful and compassionate, so should you be merciful and compassionate. (*Shabbat* 133b)

He who made the day, also made its sustenance. (*Tanhuma, Beshalah*)

Sufficient is a trouble in its hour. (*Berakhot* 9b)

Take out the splinter from your teeth. And he answered: Take out the beam from your eyes. (*Bava Batra* 15b)

It must be admitted that the similarity between the words of Jesus quoted above and the sayings of the Sages is unquestionable. As is well known, Jesus was close to the circles of the Galilean sages, and it is not hard to imagine that in his sermon he reflected the teachings of the study-halls of his time and place.

Because of the early composition of the New Testament (in the Tannaitic period) and the fairly reliable dating of its various component parts, they are valuable data for research into the literature of the Sages and its interrelations with Christianity. Later, in the Amoraic period, discussion of the interrelations between Judaism and Christianity is joined by the Church Fathers, to whom we will now turn.

The general term "Church Fathers" is usually applied to a large group of Christian writers and religious teachers who were active in various places in the Mediterranean Basin between roughly the second and the seventh century (i.e. parallel to the Amoraic period), and who developed Christian doctrines in various directions. Incidentally, one should note that the term "Fathers" as a comprehensive name for a large group of the Sages, who formulated the basic elements of Jewish doctrine, is familiar from the tractate in the Mishnah known by that name [*Avot* means "Fathers" in Hebrew], and mentioned above (see Chapter 10). Be that as it may, the works of the Church Fathers were written in several different languages: Greek, Latin, Syriac, etc., and they include works in various literary forms and having different characteristics: theological treatises, commentaries on the Bible, sermons, polemical and historiographical essays etc. Their books are full of material originating among the Jewish people and its Torah, both direct borrowings (continuing the trend we have already seen beginning in our discussion of the New Testament) and, what was more important in this period, for the requirements of rejection and polemic. The chief textual meeting-point where Christianity clashed with Judaism was, of course, in Biblical interpretation, where the Sages of Israel and the early Christians both tried to demonstrate that their way was the way of truth commanded by the Giver of the Torah.

As an example it will be sufficient to mention one of the earliest Church Fathers, Origen (185—254 C.E.). He lived in Alexandria, but often visited Caesarea in Eretz Israel where, he says, he had "a Hebrew teacher from whom he learned the language and the basic principles of Judaism." Origen wrote commentaries on the Scriptures and theological treatises, containing a defense of the new religion against its attackers. In his commentary on the Song of Songs (which was written in Greek but has reached us mainly in a

133

Latin translation) he sees the book as having two aspects: the historical one, in which the book describes the history of the relations between God and Israel, and the spiritual one, according to which the book is a poem of abstract love between the human soul and the spirit of God. To a great extent Origen is here following in the footsteps of the Sages, who saw the Song of Songs as a poetic and allegorical description of the relationship between God and the congregation of Israel. It is reasonable to assume that it was this conception which enabled the book, which sounds like purely secular love poetry, to be included among the Scriptures. Origen replaces the congregation of Israel with the Christian Church, and in this way subordinates to his own needs the accepted Jewish methods of interpretation with which he is familiar.

For example, Origen says of the first verse of the Song of Songs: "Let him kiss me with the kisses of his mouth":

The Church is the one who is speaking here and who says: I am satisfied with the gifts I have received as betrothal gifts or as a wedding dowry, for earlier, when I prepared for my wedding with the king's son... his holy angels placed themselves at my disposal, and served me by bringing me the Torah as a betrothal gift... and now I implore you to send him to me, so that he will no longer speak to me through servants, angels and prophets, but will come himself, and pour out his words face to face.

These words, the Christian character of which is clear and which contain a call for a revelation of the messiah and for regarding the Torah given at Sinai as only the first stage in creating the marriage bond between God and His beloved people, should be compared with the sermon of R. Yohanan, an Eretz Israel sage who lived in the middle of the third century, that is at the same time as Origen:

R. Yohanan explained the verse before us as speaking about Israel at the time when they went up to Mount Sinai. It was like the case of a king who wanted to marry a woman of a noble family. ...and sent an envoy to her to speak to her. She said: "... I want to hear it from his [the king's] mouth." ...Thus Israel is like the noblewoman, Moses is the envoy and the king is God (*Midrash Shir Ha-Shirim Rabbah* on this verse).

134

The basic idea is the desire of the congregation of Israel for direct contact with God, without intermediaries. The words of both R. Yohanan and Origen thus depend on the same Biblical verse, and are basically identical in their allegorical interpretation of it.

One could give many other examples to demonstrate the great wealth of Jewish traditions embedded in the writings of Origen, some of which he adapts for his purpose and some which he presents unaltered, in order to attack and denigrate them. Origen's writings also contain many traditions which have not been preserved in Jewish literature, and he must, therefore, be added to the long list of sources providing evidence for the dispersion of aggadic traditions and assisting in their dating.

We will also briefly mention another Church Father, Jerome, who came to Eretz Israel in the year 386 and died there around 420 C.E. He served as the head of a monastery in Bethlehem, learned Hebrew from Jewish teachers (he even mentions one of them by name: Bar Haninah), and used this knowledge in order to translate the Bible into Latin, the translation known as the Vulgate (see Chapter 9 above). Jerome's immense knowledge of contemporary Jewish exegesis, i.e. the literature of the Sages, is also reflected in the scriptural commentaries he wrote and the many traditions he repeats in his books on the geography and history of Eretz Israel.

We are still waiting for a book which will list methodically and concisely all the traditions known to us from the literature of the Sages which also appear in the prolific literature of the Church Fathers. Origen, for example, knows the tradition that Job was a contemporary of Moses, while Jerome is able to say that Isaac "went out to stroll in the field" (Genesis 24:63) in order to pray. Another Church Father, Ephrem the Syrian (306—373) said that Nadav and Avihu, the sons of Aaron, entered the Tabernacle when they were drunk and were killed by a fire which came from the Holy of Holies. All these traditions and many others like them are familiar to us from the literature of the Sages, and were almost certainly derived from it, either orally or through writing. The fact that we can date the Church Fathers with certainty is, as mentioned, a useful tool for research into the history of these traditions.

135

Early Christian literature also assists us to a better understanding of the midrashim. Urbach gives an instructive example of this. The Jerusalem Talmud claims that: "the repentance of the people of Nineveh was insincere" (*Ta'anit* 2:5). This means that they pretended to repent, but in fact only wanted to deceive. This is in almost open contradiction to the spirit of what is written in the Book of Jonah (the reading of which in the afternoon prayer of *Yom Kippur* is almost certainly based on the assumption that the repentance of Nineveh was genuine). It also contradicts what is said in the Mishnah, which sees the penitence of the people of Nineveh as something worthy of imitation. According to the Mishnah (*Ta'anit* 2:1), at a time of drought the people should be encouraged to scrutinize their deeds and to turn from their evil ways, using as an example the story of the sinful men of Nineveh, who were saved from death by their repentance. What, then, led the Jerusalem Talmud to turn the Biblical story almost completely upside down? In Urbach's opinion, this contradiction arises from the requirements of an anti-Christian polemic, for, as we have already seen in the quotation from the New Testament, Christianity turned the behavior of the Gentiles of Nineveh into an example, and saw it as proof of the possibility that a Gentile and a foreigner could in fact come to know the truth, while a Jew, a member of Jonah's own people, could ignore God's call to change his ways. In order to prevent the Christians from using this story to attack Judaism, the Sages of Israel, who conducted a bitter and acrimonious dispute with Christianity, changed their interpretation of the Biblical story. This is a good example of the contribution which research on the writings of the Church Fathers can make to a fuller understanding of the Sages. We have already had occasion to remark (Chapter 1, above) on the great importance of Judeo-Christian controversy in the history of aggadic literature.

Judaism and Christianity, as mother and daughter, or as sister religions, strove together for a very long time, and this struggle left its traces in their writings and their literature. Our picture of the world of the Sages will be complete only if this fact is always taken into account.

XII.

Samaritan and Muslim Literature

Apart from early Christianity, two other literatures and cultures should be mentioned, both of which are also early and have a very well-known relationship with the literature of the Sages: Samaritan and Muslim literature.

The Samaritans have a varied literary heritage: prayers, liturgical poetry and songs, in Hebrew, Aramaic and Arabic; historiographical works dealing mainly with their own history; books on religious subjects like halachah, customs and polemics on various questions; books on language and grammar, such as dictionaries; commentaries on the Torah, and a translation of it into Samaritan Aramaic. Naturally, all of these also bear the stamp of Jewish culture, the neighbor and rival of Samaritan culture, for, apart from the fact that the two lived side by side for centuries, they both had a firm common foundation — belief in the Torah of Moses and study of it.

The most important books for the Samaritans were evidently the Torah (in the version that became sanctified among them, which is not identical in every detail with that accepted in Judaism) and its translation into Samaritan Aramaic. As is well known, at the time of their final separation from Judaism, the Samaritans did not adopt the books of the Prophets or the Hagiographa, and granted only the Book of Joshua a special status. Third in rank among their literature — and the Samaritans themselves would evidently agree with this judgment — is the work of a sage called Merqe, a Palestinian of the

137

third to fourth century. This book, written in Samaritan Aramaic, is called *Meimar Merqe*, and is a kind of midrash on part of the Torah, a midrash mixed with some interpretation and with many digressions into various subjects, as well as additions and expansions of a philosophical, theological or didactic nature. In dealing with the part of the Torah story between the burning bush and the death of Moses (we will see later why he chose to discuss this particular section), Merqe combines religious beliefs, interpretation, hymns, preaching etc., and in this way provides us with a rich anthology of Samaritan traditions contemporary with the Palestinian Amoraim. Very many of these traditions were derived from Jewish sources, or reached both Merqe and the Sages, in writing or orally, from earlier literature, such as the apocryphal writings (discussed in Chapter 2 above).

Here is an example of the connection between the midrashim of the Sages and Merqe. When Pharaoh's army is drawing close to the Israelites, Moses says to them:

> Stand still, and see the salvation of the Lord... for the Egyptians whom you have seen today, you will see them again no more for ever. The Lord will fight for you, and you will hold your peace. (Exodus 14:13—14)

On this Merqe says:

> Beside the sea the Israelites divided into three groups. Each group said something, and was answered by the great prophet [Moses]. The first group said, "Let us return to Egypt and work for them." And Moses said to them, "You will see them again no more for ever." The second group said, "Let us flee from the Egyptians into the desert." Moses said to them, "Stand still, and see the salvation of the Lord." The third group said, "Let us rise up and fight against the Egyptians." Moses said to them, "The Lord will fight for you, and you will hold your peace."

This version, telling of the division of the people into three sections according to three different types of people addressed in Moses' detailed words of reassurance, seems to be earlier than the tradition documented in Tannaitic literature, according to which Moses addressed four groups:

138

Israel divided into four groups beside the sea. One said to fall into the sea; one said to return to Egypt; one said to make war against them; and one said, "Let us scream against them." (*Mekhilta Beshalah* 2)

In this tradition as well, Moses answers each group's suggestion. He replies to the last group, the one that says, "Let us scream against them," by saying, "Hold your peace." In the tradition documented by Merqe, three suggestions for dealing with the situation are current among the people: fighting the Egyptians, flight from the field of battle, or unconditional surrender. But someone evidently wanted to consider the words "The Lord will fight for you, and you will hold your peace" as two separate answers by Moses, addressed to two separate groups and, to correspond with "you will hold your peace," he invented a fourth group, whose suggestion, "Let us scream " seems rather artificial. (I do not think "Let us scream" should be interpreted as a suggestion to pray to God for help. For why should Moses reject this idea?) The tradition given by Merqe seems, therefore, to be the original, and so the *Meimar Merqe* is also among the important works that can help us to date traditions in the literature of the Sages and even provide information on their history and development.

When Merqe describes Moses and Aaron as coming to Egypt together after their meeting on the Mountain of God in the desert (*Exodus* 4:27), he breaks into this song:

How wonderful to see them entering Egypt
Like the two angels coming to Sodom.
The two angels entered Sodom with the evening,
Sent to open a store of wrath on all its citizens.
Moses and Aaron entered Egypt with the evening,
Sent to open a store of judgment [punishment] upon it.
The two angels were sent to demolish Sodom,
And Moses and Aaron were sent to demolish Egypt.
The two angels ate unleavened bread in Sodom,
And Moses and Aaron celebrated the feast of unleavened bread in Egypt.
The two angels led out Lot in the morning,

And Moses and Aaron first let out Israel in the morning. The two will be honored for ever; their greatness fills the heavens and the earth.

I have not succeeded in finding a parallel to this detailed analogy between the entry of Moses and Aaron to Egypt and the coming of the angels to Lot while he was living in Sodom. Nor have I found any tradition which specifically states that it was in the evening that Moses and Aaron came to Egypt. But in dealing with the history of traditions it is important to remember that lack of evidence is no evidence to the contrary, and while it is possible that Merqe, who was also a well-known poet, was the creator and originator of this tradition, it is also possible that he heard some of the things he puts into his book from Jews, or read them in their writings.

The fact that Merqe writes about Moses need not surprise us. Moses won a special place in Samaritan theology. As mentioned above, the books of the Prophets were not considered sacred by the Samaritans, and the belief in Moses as the one, single prophet was one of the principles of their religion, like their belief in one God and his Torah and in the sanctity of Mount Gerizim. The messianic figure in the Samaritan faith, who is called "Tahav" (i.e. one who comes back, returns, and gives back), will, in a way be a "prophet like Moses," and will, like him, be active for forty years. For these reasons particular attention was paid to Moses in Samaritan literature, and this is demonstrated by the special position he assumes in Merqe's writings.

Here it is worth noting that the fact that Moses occupies this central position in Samaritan thinking — especially when we add to it the image of Jesus as the second Moses in early Christianity — is sufficient to explain why Moses did not achieve the position of a messianic figure in Judaism. The Prophet Elijah, King David, the Messiah, the Son of Joseph, and others all play an important role in the world to come, but not Moses. This is surprising, for it would be reasonable to assume that popular imagination would expect the one who redeemed the people at the beginning of history to be the one to return and redeem it at the End of Days. But in fact Moses does not play this role in the literature of the Sages (except in a few isolated and obscure sources), and has no part in the picture of future redemption. He does not even appear in the Passover Haggadah, a work which glorifies the story of past redemption and looks forward to redemption in the future. These Samaritan and Christian ideas about Moses apparently compelled Judaism to play down any messianic dimension which had been attributed to him and to restrict him to the status of a past redeemer alone.

Another Samaritan work, the *Book of Asatir*, written in Aramaic, also devotes much space to Moses. This book is a chronicle relating the history of the world from the Creation until Moses, concentrating on Adam, Noah, Abraham and Moses, as well as a description of the borders of the Land of Israel and visions of the future. The book was written in the Muslim period (incidentally, *asatir* means "stories" in Arabic), and in the course of time was attributed to Moses himself. It contains much material which accumulated around Biblical stories, and naturally in part parallels Jewish sources, and was perhaps even derived from them.

For example, in describing the journey down to Egypt by Abraham and Sarah (Genesis 12), the author of the *Book of Asatir* says:

> And at once Abraham went down to Egypt ... and there the women saw Sarah and praised her to the men, and the men [did so] to Pharaoh, and the woman was taken to Pharaoh's house (v. 15). And while Sarah was in Pharaoh's house, many marvels were revealed, and Pharaoh was like a stone [i.e. he was struck dumb]... and among the magicians was a seer called Tortes ... and he said, "There is in this place a worshipper of the universal God [referring to Abraham], and all this trouble is on account of him" ... Then Sarah told them she was Abraham's wife, and Pharaoh's tongue was released and he spoke, and Abraham prayed and asked for salvation... and immediately Pharaoh was healed...

We will discuss two of the motifs which the author adds to the Biblical story. (Compare also the treatment of this story in the Genesis Apocryphon, Chapter 5 above.) In the Biblical story, "the Egyptians beheld the woman that she was very fair... the princes of

141

Pharaoh saw her, and praised her before Pharaoh..." (vs. 14—15), while our author stresses Sarah's modesty by stating that it was only the women who saw her and described her beauty to the men. This tendency to intensify Sarah's modesty (particularly in a rather problematic story like this one) is common to many sources in the literature of the Sages. In some of them Sarah was so modest that even Abraham her husband did not know how beautiful she was, and it was only when her figure was reflected in the waters of the Nile that he saw her reflection and learned what her face looked like. According to another tradition, he learned of her beauty from the Egyptians who spoke about her. I have not found another tradition identical with that of the *Book of Asatir*, and it is possible that it reflects the accepted customs of the society in which the author grew up. On the other hand, in some places the author adorns the story of Abraham and Sarah in Egypt with details he has taken from the parallel Biblical story, the story of Abraham and Sarah in Gerar (Genesis 20). Both stories, of course, say that Sarah pretended to be Abraham's sister, and in both stories she is taken to the king's palace and is saved by the intervention of God. The author of the *Book of Asatir* transfers from the Gerar story to the Egypt story the detail that Pharaoh's punishment was remitted only when Abraham prayed for him (cf. Genesis 20:17), and relying on this he permits himself not to tell his readers that Pharaoh gave Abraham many gifts when he took his wife (Genesis 12:16), for this is something which does not appear in Genesis 20. (In this story the gifts are given to Abraham and Sarah when she is returned to her husband as compensation, not in payment for her.) The tendency to paint a Biblical story in colors taken from another Biblical story, whether a similar one or not, is very common in the literature of the Sages, and in this respect the Samaritan work we are discussing is very similar in its methods of treatment and in subject matter to what is found in ancient Jewish sources, whether it was directly derived from them or merely following after them.

The relationship between the literature of the Sages and Samaritan literature finds particular expression in the controversy between the two sister religions, controversy which centered on the question of the sanctity of Mount Gerizim among others, but this question — like that of the Judeo-Christian controversy — deserves fuller treatment, and this is not the place for it.

The relationship between Jewish culture and Muslim literature in the early Middle Ages did not begin only at the moment when Islam burst forth from the Arabian peninsula and in a storm of conquest overran considerable parts of the civilized world of the time (around the year 635 C.E.). It is certainly true that from the time when Eretz Israel and Babylon came under the yoke of the Muslims, whose religion was not so very different from that of the Jews, the literary and ideological links between the two religions were strengthened and tightened, but these links originated in the pre-Islamic period (known as the *Jahiliyah*). Muhammad, the prophet and originator of the new religion, acquired a great deal of information from Christians and Jews, both permanent residents of the Arabian peninsula and transient merchants, and embedded them in many places in the Muslim holy book, the Koran.

This book gave the Muslim faith its shape and established its theoretical and practical basis. It is divided into chapters (*Suras* in Arabic), which, not always methodically, treat various questions, including the stories of Muhammad's predecessors, who were considered by him as prophets: Adam, Noah, the Patriarchs, Ishmael, Joseph, Moses, David, Solomon, Jesus and others. These stories should be our main interest because the traces of Jewish and Christian culture, from which the Prophet of Islam derived these stories, can be easily detected in them.

Scholars are divided over the question of the nature of Muhammad's expertise in Jewish and Christian literature and the extent of his socio-cultural links with the Jewish community in the south of the Arabian peninsula (the roots of which go back perhaps to the Biblical period itself). Some scholars think that Muhammad absorbed vast amounts of Jewish (and Christian) sources from thorough reading and study, while others think that his knowledge of these matters was in the main acquired by ear, superficially and unsystematically, without his being able to understand fully their deeper meaning. Be that as it may, the fact is that there are dozens of places in the Koran which reveal clear links with obviously Jewish traditions, apart from the basic principles of the Islamic religion (such as the eternity and the oneness of God, the importance of prayer, pilgrimage, purification, charity and similar matters), whose connections between Islam and the earlier monotheistic religions are self-evident.

For example, *Sura 2 (33—35)* says:

> God said: "Adam, dwell you and your wife in the Garden of Eden and eat [of the fruit] thereof plentifully wherever you will; but approach not this tree, lest you become of [the number of] the transgressors." But Satan caused them to fail and drove them out of the place wherein they had been... And Adam learned words from God, and returned to Him, for He is forgiving and merciful.

For this, Muhammad depends, of course, on the story of Adam and Eve in the Garden of Eden, but also on other, post-Biblical Jewish traditions, like the one which identifies the serpent with Satan, or the one which states that Adam repented and was forgiven: "The Lord opened a door to repentance for him," says one midrash (*Bereshit Rabbah* 21:6), for "God suggested to Adam that he should repent" (*Tanhuma* [Buber], *Tazria* 11).

Among the topics in the Koran deserving of comment, one of the most significant is the particular use Muhammad made of the figure of Haman. He transferred this enemy of the Jews to the Egyptian period and made him Pharaoh's chief counsellor and first minister. This is what it says in the Koran:

> We [the speaker is God] have already sent Moses with our signs and in open authority to Pharaoh and to Haman and Korah, and they said, "Moses is only a magician and a teller of lies!" And when Moses came to them in truth from Us, they said, "Put the sons of the Believers [the Israelite children] to death together with him, and leave only their daughters alive."

This is evidently a combination of the Biblical story of Pharaoh's order to put the Israelite children to death and the story in the Book of Esther of Haman's wish to destroy, to kill and to exterminate the entire Jewish people. This mixture, which is either to be blamed on those who carried Jewish traditions to the south of the Arabian peninsula, or was an innovation by Muhammad himself, is apparently also connected with a common midrashic tradition which states that Pharaoh had three counsellors who advised him to give the order: "Every son that is born, you will cast into the river" (See *Shemot Rabbah* 1:12). There the counsellors are Balaam, Job and Jethro. One should also remember another midrashic tradition which associates Haman and Korah: "There were two rich men in the world... Korah from Israel and Haman from the nations of the world" (*Bemidbar Rabbah* 22:6 and elsewhere). It appears, therefore, that Biblical stories and various post-Biblical traditions were combined in Muhammad's version, and thus a new tradition was created, one which Muhammad presented to his followers as an example of arrogance, wickedness and excessive pride.

Examples of this kind can be multiplied. They all combine to demonstrate the dispersion of Jewish traditions at the beginning of the seventh century, even to the most remote areas of that time, and the variations in their transmission. When discussing literature produced up to the seventh century, in most cases the direction of the borrowing is clear: from Judaism and Christianity to the originator and Prophet of Islam, but when dealing with traditions which appear in Hebrew literature written from the eighth century onwards, the position is more complicated, since it is always possible that the Koran contributed something to Jewish literature, while there are also various connections between Jewish traditions and the Muslim literature which flourished after the Koran was written: commentaries on the Koran (*tafsir*), historical works (*ta'arikh*), and oral traditions (*hadith*) about the Prophet and his disciples.

One work included among the midrashic literature which is particularly notable for its links with Islam is known as the *Chapters of R. Eliezer*. It was apparently written in the eighth century (its attribution to the Tanna R. Eliezer has no historical foundation), and there is much in it which has clear links with Muslim literature and culture (such as the statement, which also appears in the Koran, that Pharaoh did not drown in the Sea of Reeds).

For example, the anonymous author of this book writes (ch. 30): Ishmael sent and took a wife from the wilderness of Moab, and her name was Isa. Three years later Abraham went to see Ishmael, his son. And he swore to Sarah that he would not get down from his camel in the place where Ishmael was dwelling. He arrived there at mid-day, and found Ishmael's wife there. He said to her, "Where is Ishmael?" She said to him, "He has gone with his mother [Hagar] to bring fruit and dates from the desert." He said to her, "Give me a little bread and water, for my spirit is weary from the journey in the desert." She said to him, "I have no bread and no water." He said to her, "When Ishmael comes, tell him these words and say to him that an old man came from the Land of Canaan to see you, and say that the threshold of the house [here this is a poetic expression for a woman] is not good." When he came, his wife told him these things. He divorced her, and his mother sent and took another wife for him from her father's house, and her name was Fatima. Three years later Abraham came again... [and again met Ishmael's wife]... and he said to her, "Give me a little bread and a little water, for my spirit is weary from the journey in the desert." She brought it out and gave it to him. Abraham stood and prayed to the Lord for his son, and Ishmael's house was filled with all good things through the blessings. And when Ishmael came, his wife told him these things, and Ishmael knew that his father was still merciful towards him.

The names Fatima and Isa are familiar to us from sources on the life of the Prophet of Islam (see Chapter 9 above). The first was his daughter and the second one of his wives. It is clear that the author wants to present Ishmael as archetype of the prophet of the new faith, and so he describes him with characteristics taken from the biography of Muhammad, even if these are not accurate, but mistakenly gives the wife the daughter's name. Scholars are divided over the origins of the story: some say that it is an original Jewish story, while others regard it as Muslim in origin.

Whatever the case may be, the *Chapters of R. Eliezer* displays a particular attitude towards Islam, an attitude which is both polemical and at the same time apologetic. On the one hand the book engages in polemics with the new faith in stating that Abraham did not descend from his camel and did not pay his son a real visit (this is a subtle polemic against the Muslim traditions that one place or another in the Arabian peninsula was in fact sanctified by Abraham). On the other hand he speaks of Abraham's love for his son, of his longing for him and of his prayers on his behalf.

Moreover, it gives the following etymology for Ishmael's name: "That God will hearken to the moaning of the people [of Israel] over what the children of Ishmael are destined to do." (ch. 33) [Ishmael means "God will hear" in Hebrew.] On the other hand, the book claims, in clear and open contradiction to many sources of the Tannaic and Amoraic periods, that Ishmael did not worship idols, for Islam was in fact not considered as idolatry.

★

The aggadic literature of the Sages — as we have seen over and over again — was not a "literature standing alone," and in almost every period it sent out its tendrils among the branches of all the literatures and cultures of the time, Muslim, Samaritan and Christian literatures from without, literature of the Dead Sea sect, of the mystics and others from within; all of these comprise the correct background for seeing the aggadic literature of the Sages in its true form and nature.

BIBLIOGRAPHY

S. Lieberman, *Greek in Jewish Palestine*, New York, 1942.

----------, *Hellenism in Jewish Palestine*, New York, 1950.

J. Neusner, *What is Midrash?*, Philadelphia, 1987.

G.G. Porton, *Understanding Rabbinic Midrash*, Hoboken, NJ, 1985.

E.E. Urbach, *The Sages — Their Concepts and Beliefs*, Jerusalem, 1975.

G. Vermes, *Scripture and Tradition in Judaism*, Leiden, 1973.